Colchester Memories

PATRICK DENNEY

AMBERLEY

Acknowledgements

It goes without saying that I owe a great debt of gratitude to the many people who have been kind enough to share their memories with me in the first place, because without their assistance such a book would not have been possible. The same is true with respect to the many illustrations that have been used to supplement the text and my thanks is due to the many unknown photographers whose work is here included, as well as to the late Bill Tucker for his lovely cartoon included on page 6. I would also like to express my thanks to the following individuals who have kindly made available treasured family photographs and other archive material in support of the publication: Jacki Barber, Tony Blaxill, Joy Cardy, Mike Davies, Peter Evans, Mary Garner, Alan Garnett, Dennis Golby, Phil Gunton, Hugh Harvey, Olive Hazel, Jess Jephcott, Peter Jones, David Judge, Pauline and Jim Lawrence, Dennis Marchant, Andrew Phillips, Fred Rayner, Amanda Sancassani, Reg Shelley, Janet and David Snow, Jill Thorogood, Joan and Jim Watson, Brian Webb and Gordon Williams.

If I have made any omissions, or failed to identify the copyright owner of any of the illustrations included, it is with regret and I offer my apologies.

For Jess, Anna and Joe

First published 2014

Amberley Publishing
The Hill, Stroud
Gloucestershire, GL5 4EP

www.amberley-books.com

British Library Cataloguing in Publication Data.
A catalogue record for this book is available from the British Library.

ISBN 978 1 4456 1854 8 (print)
ISBN 978 1 4456 1873 9 (ebook)

Typeset in 10pt on 12pt Sabon.
Typesetting and Origination by Amberley Publishing.
Printed in the UK.

Contents

Introduction

This book is very much a sequel to my previous title, *Colchester Voices*, and once again taps into the rich memories and knowledge of local residents, both past and present – past in the sense that since I began recording these memories back in the late 1980s, many of the people interviewed are sadly no longer with us. A total of forty-five individuals feature in this present volume, around half of whom were born before 1920, a few in the 1920s and the remainder during the 1930s and 1940s. The interviews were completed over a period of more than twenty years in two distinct stages, with the older group completed during the period 1989–2000 and the younger group between 2000 and 2013.

The oldest person featured in the book was born in 1889 and was interviewed shortly after her 100th birthday. She was able to vividly recall events from the early years of the twentieth century, including seeing the first motor car in Colchester. At the other end of the scale, the youngest participant, born as recently as 1947, provides us with an insight into life in the 'swinging sixties'.

Many aspects of life are featured in the selected extracts, including memories of growing up in an age without modern conveniences, and at a time when you had to make your own entertainment rather than watching television or playing video games. The section dealing with occupations and trade includes memories of what it was like working on the land using horse power, as well as factory and shop work long before the age of modern superstores and labour saving machinery. But perhaps some of the most poignant memories recalled belong to those who both fought and lived during the turbulent years of war. This was particularly true in the case of those who experienced life on the Home Front during the Second World War, whose memories of the period were recalled with extreme clarity more than fifty or sixty years later.

Collectively, the interviews form part of a much larger archive assembled by the Colchester Recalled Oral History Group, which itself stands as a valuable contribution to our knowledge and understanding of local life in the early to mid-twentieth century. The varied extracts chosen for inclusion in the book are representative of that archive as a whole and will allow the reader to gain a real insight and flavour of a period in our recent history that is fast disappearing, if not already lost.

Patrick Denney
2014

Chapter One

Home & Family

We Were Not on the Sewer

I was born at 86 Hythe Hill and the rent was 7/6d a week. We were not on the sewer and there were two privies down the garden for us and the house next door. There was one high seat and one low seat for the children and they would be emptied once a week. My mother used to leave 6d on the seat for the night soil man who came to empty them. We had a cold tap in the kitchen for all our water, and for lighting we had candles and oil lamps. Later on we had gas lamps, but it was just a naked flame.

Nellie Lissimore (born 1889)

A Bath in the Kitchen

We lived in a three-bedroomed house in Wimpole Road. There was no bathroom and every week my mother would light the copper to heat the water to give us a bath. I had two brothers and two sisters and mother would bath us in the kitchen in a tin bath. I had to sleep with my sisters and the two boys slept in another room, while my mother and father had the front room. We had an outside toilet and just round the corner from that was a little sheltered area where we would throw all our rubbish. The dustmen used to shovel it up in a sack and put it on a horse and cart.

Dorothy Lawrence (born 1897)

A typical two-hole privy that may have been emptied once a week, or perhaps even once a year, depending on its type and construction.

Friday Night Was Bath Night

Friday night was bath night and we used to sit in front of the fire in a tin bath. The girls went in first so their hair got dry and the boys afterwards. We used to have some fun and then we'd play up the devil when we got to bed. Mother would stand at the bottom of the stairs and say, 'I'll be up there after you in a minute if you don't shut up!'

Margaret Golby (born 1901)

We Had to Pay a Shilling for a Bath

We used to have to bath in a tub in front of the fire. The water was boiled up in a copper, which was in the kitchen. When I got older and went to work, I used to go to Beaumont's shop in Culver Street and have a bath there. We had to pay about a shilling (5p) a time, although most people used to bathe at home.

Doris Thimblethorpe (born 1903)

Three at the Top of the Bed and Three at the Bottom

My mother had ten children at home in a two-bedroomed house. We used to sleep three at the top of the bed and three at the bottom. My father used to work on the land for 11s a week (55p), but then he got a job at the gasworks where he earned 17s (85p) and he thought he was a millionaire. He was a stoker and worked a twelve-hour shift, seven days a week.

Ernie Went (born 1905)

We Used to Catch Sparrows in a Trap

When I was a young lad living in Granville Road, we used to catch sparrows in a trap. You'd have a large tray propped up with a stick attached to a bit of string, with some breadcrumbs under there, and then when they got underneath you'd pull the stick away. We used to pluck them and bake them in the oven. We used to eat the bones and everything. Dinner time was twelve o'clock. You couldn't get up to the table 'til you were told, and you couldn't get down from the table 'til you were told. And if you were to use the knife and fork the wrong way, you would

Bath night was a family affair.

get a whack from father's stick. We never had Quaker Oats or anything like that in my childhood. We just had some bread and margarine for breakfast and that was that. If you didn't want it, you wouldn't get anything else.

Albert Hewitt (born 1903)

Sunday Was a Special Day

Sunday was a special day at home. I wasn't allowed to read the newspaper or anything like that. We used to have to go to church morning, afternoon and evening. We would wear special Sunday clothes, which hadn't been worn on a weekday. My parents were not overly strict but they were Christian parents. They knelt and said their prayers before going to bed every night.

Ivy Green (born 1906)

Mother Would Use Gunpowder to Light the Copper

We had a copper in the kitchen for the washing, which was a big brick affair with a small place for a fire. I used to have to go up to Howe's the gunsmiths in Long Wyre Street and buy some gunpowder, which mother would use to start the fire. She would put a little of this gunpowder in a piece of paper and put that under the copper. She would then put the poker in the front to blow it up to start it off. I suppose that would be thought of as dangerous today, but they did it at that time of day.

Albert Bridges (born 1908)

Mother Used to Sprinkle Tea Leaves on the Carpet

We had a living room, a sitting room and a kitchen, but no bathroom. I can remember that my mother used to sprinkle tea leaves over the carpet when she swept it because it kept the dust down. And when anybody was ill in bed they used

Ivy Green, pictured in 1990, aged eighty-four.

Nellie Lissimore in 1989, aged 100.

to put straw down in the road to quieten the noise of the traffic. And if somebody died, people would put a black board in their window – I'm not sure whether this was provided by the undertakers or not.

Nellie Lissimore (born 1889)

Everybody Drew Their Curtains as a Mark of Respect
When a funeral was taking place in a road, everybody drew their curtains as a mark of respect. And if somebody had died in business, the shop, or premises, would put up a black board signifying that somebody had died. I can also remember walking along Osborne Street with my mother and seeing some straw in the road, and my mother telling me that this was because somebody was very ill and they were trying to prevent the noise of the wheels on the roadway from disturbing them.

Alice Twyman (born 1906)

When a Funeral Came Past You Took Your Hat Off
I remember one time when the man who lived next door to us was very ill and they had straw laid over the path and road so the horse and carts didn't make a noise. And if anyone in the street died, you'd all put a black board up at your windows. Everybody wore black and when the funeral came past, you'd take your hat off.

Albert Hewitt (born 1903)

Times Were Very Hard
During the slump in the 1920s, my father was out of work for more than two years. Times were very hard and often we were waiting for the gas man to come and empty the meter and give us a refund of a few pennies. My mother did sewing and cleaning work and somehow managed to keep us fed and warm.

Les Beagen (born 1910)

Everything Had to Go Through the Wringer
The weekly wash used to last for three or four days. Monday was washing day and we had a big copper in the kitchen, which you boiled the clothes in. You then took the water and clothes out of the copper and put them in a big galvanised bath. We

then had a thing called a scrubbing board and, with some Sunlight soap, you rubbed it on the clothes up and down on this scrubbing board to get them clean. Then came the job of rinsing in cold water, after which they were put through a mangle to get the water out. When we did the 'whites' you would add a solution called 'Dolly Blue', which made the whites whiter. After all that it was put out on the line. When it was dry, everything had to go through the mangle again to take the creases out. Then, of course, came the ironing. Everything was ironed with irons heated on the fire – the old cast-iron flat irons. With all this washing, rinsing, drying and ironing, most people never got through it until Wednesday.

Albert Cork (born 1911)

My Mother Would Be Washing Until Two o'clock in the Morning
My mother used to take in washing when my father died. Monday was washing day and she would heat the water up in the copper, which was next to the sink. For whitening the linen, we would have to use what they called a 'Blue Bag', which made the water blue, and you rinsed everything in that. She would rinse everything in a tin bath on a stool. And when the linen had been washed it was put through a mangle in the kitchen. It would then be hung out to dry – I can see the old line full of linen now. Sometimes my mother would be standing there washing until two o'clock in the morning, before she would just have to drop everything and go to bed. And then all this washing had to be ironed with a goffering iron. She only got paid about five bob (25p) for doing all this washing.

Margaret Golby (born 1901)

We Used to Take a Candle Up to the Bedroom
For lighting, I can first remember there being a big brass chandelier paraffin lamp hanging from the ceiling. We had one in each room except for the kitchen, where we had candles. Years later, we had gas lights, which were a lot better, and then after that we got electric lights, which were better still. When I was young they used to have gas lights in the streets and gas lighters would come round to light the lamps. They had a carbide container on a long pole and they used to go round the streets lighting the lamps with that. They would first come round when it started to get dark, and then come round again at about twelve o'clock at night to put them out.

Albert Bridges (born 1908)

The Tramps Would Swear at Us
When we first got married, we lived in Crowhurst Road, not far from the workhouse. When the tramps came out in the morning they would call at various houses asking for some hot water. Then if you gave them some hot water, they would want some sugar as well, and if you didn't give it to them they would swear at you. Very often, they would ask for some bread and butter and if you gave them something that they didn't want, they would throw it down in the road.

Doris Thimblethorpe (born 1903)

We Used to Empty the Toilet on the Garden
We never had a bathroom. Mother used to bath us in a metal bath on Saturday nights. She used to heat the water in a copper. The toilet was outside down the yard. It had two seats – a 'biggin' and a 'littlin' for the children. We used to empty

St Mary's Hospital, formerly Colchester Union Workhouse.

them every year onto the garden and dig it in. We used to empty them ourselves, everybody used to do the same. We used to dig it in where we had greens and that, but not where we had potatoes. We didn't have any water in the house. There was a well down at Crockleford Heath and it used to supply about four or five houses. I'm still on well water where I live now. We used to have to put the pail down the well using a chrome – that's a long pole with a snap thing on the end – and you put the handle of the pail on the snap and then dropped the pail down the well, and deaved it down and brought the water up.

Ernie Went (born 1905)

I Used to Buy a Ha'penny Worth of Stickjaw
My dad used to give me a ha'penny (half a penny) pocket money when he came home from work, and I used go to Cater's shop, which was next to our school, to buy a ha'pence worth of stickjaw. It was a type of rock, because Cater's were rock makers, and it was like a brown toffee, made in trays, and when you were eating you couldn't speak because it would stick to your mouth. We used to get it when we were having needlework lessons at school because we were not allowed to speak in class. I also used to earn some pocket money by going round collecting rents for a neighbour called Mrs Perry. She used to own about five houses in the area, for which she would charge about 7/6d each a week rent. She also ran a dairy and her son used to come round delivering the milk in cans on a barrow, and that was how we got our milk.

Ivy Green (born 1906)

East Hill looking up towards the town centre, with Cater's confectionery shop on the right.

Charles Perry with his mobile milk churn.

My Sister Was Given a Good Hiding

In Spurgeon Street, where all the doors are close together, we used to tie up two neighbours' door handles with a piece of string, then bang on the door and run away. Well, one day the piece of string came off one of the houses and my eldest sister got caught and was given a good hiding. My mother couldn't say anything and said, 'Good job, they shouldn't have done it.'

Elsie Seaborne (born 1906)

We Had to Say Grace at Mealtimes

Our parents were not overly strict, but if we didn't behave ourselves our father would give us a rap on the head. We had to say grace at mealtimes and we were not allowed to leave the table without his permission. On the odd occasion when we were out playing, we were not beyond cheeking PC Clarke, the local policeman, and he would sting us round the ears with his gloves if he caught us. And then if he told my father I got another hiding.

Dick Thorogood (born 1911)

The Doctor Used to Call Round in a Horse and Cart

Our family doctor was Doctor Worts, who used to come round in his horse and cart. On one occasion, my little sister Hannah had to have her tonsils out and the doctor did the operation at home. Mother had to clear the bedroom and scrub the table and everything was put out of the room. The doctor took her tonsils out and then my mother had to look after her. When we used to have a Sunday school treat, a coal cart was scrubbed out, boards were put across, and us kids used to sit on these boards and they would take us to the Castle Park – that was our Sunday school treat.

Margaret Golby (born 1901)

Nobody Dared to Lift a Spade on a Sunday

Sunday in Rowhedge was a very quiet day. The place was really asleep. Nobody dared to lift a spade in the garden. And you would never hang your washing out on a Sunday. At ten o'clock we would go to Sunday school, then at eleven o'clock you left Sunday School and went up to church. We left church at 12.30 p.m. and went home for some lunch, and then by 2.30 p.m. we were back at Sunday school again. After that, we came out and most people would go for a walk in Donyland Woods before going back to church again in the evening, where I was in the choir. We would come out at eight o'clock and make our way home. That was Sunday.

Albert Cork (born 1911)

I Got a Penny a Week Pocket Money

I had to do my fair share of chores when I was at home. I'd have to clean father's shed, or clean the knives and forks, do the brasses and anything else. I got a penny a week pocket money for that, which I'd spend on sweets. We used to go to Steggles shop and you could buy a big carrot for a ha'penny, and perhaps a ha'penny worth of sweets. They never put the sweets into bags in those days, but used to roll them up in a sheet of newspaper.

Albert Hewitt (born 1903)

All the Family Used to Go to Chapel

Our family was a bit religious and we used to go to the chapel just next door – the whole family would go, mother, father and children. We went to Sunday school in the morning at nine o'clock, then we would have dinner and go back to the chapel in the afternoon. The chapel would be right full. I've played the violin in there for seventy years – I still play now. I got my first violin from Mann's shop in Colchester. I gave 30s for it and I've still got it. A string for it costs more than that now. I started playing when I was about sixteen, both me and my brother Arthur, we bought one each. It took us about a year to learn how to play it. Looking back, there was more contentment years ago than there is today. People today are never satisfied. People didn't do anything on a Sunday other than go for a walk. We used to walk for miles but they wouldn't do it today. It was much safer then, you could leave your door unlocked all night, but you wouldn't do it now.

Ernie Went (born 1905)

The Milk Was Delivered by Donkey and Trap

The milk used to be delivered in a donkey and trap. The milkman used to go all the way over to Fingringhoe to collect his milk and then bring it over to Rowhedge. Of course, it was in the churn and was sold in those days by ladling it out in a standard half or one pint measure. There was no pasteurisation or anything like that – it was straight from the cow to the churn and from the churn to your jug. Sometimes we would walk up to Battleswick Farm to get our milk. They had a dairy in the house and we would get our milk direct from them. It was that much cheaper and fresh from the cow.

Albert Cork (born 1911)

George and Hannah Went and their thirteen children, c. 1920. Ernie is pictured on the left in the back row wearing a trilby, while to the right in the back row, also wearing a trilby, is his brother Arthur.

It Was Quite an Operation When the Sweep Came

We only ever had a coal fire in the living room and there was no heating in any of the bedrooms, unless someone was ill in bed, when a fire would be lit. The front room was never used except on special occasions, such as Christmas. It was quite an operation when Mr Ramplin, the sweep, would come to clean the chimneys. The rooms had to be cleared out and other things covered up as the coal dust and soot got everywhere. Most evenings at home were spent listening to the wireless or amusing ourselves by playing card games – we had no television in those days. We would all sit in the same room listening and playing.

Basil Smith (born 1924)

Friday Night Was Bath Night

When my parents moved to Colchester when I was little, my father got a job with the council and was offered the tenancy of a new council house in Wick Road. It was a regular council house with outdoor loo, but it was within the building. And we had a coal bunker inside the house – I can remember that. We also had a downstairs bathroom, but we had to heat the water in a copper. Friday night was bath night and we all had to use that water. You lit a fire under the copper to boil the water and then ladled it into the bath. On Monday, the copper was lit again to do the washing, because Monday was wash day. I remember that we had a big mangle with two big rollers and as you turned the handle these rollers moved.

Hugh Harvey (born 1932)

Hugh Harvey and his young playmate, Joy Fisher.

We Had to Go to Town for a Bath

When I was about seven years old, we moved from our house in Goring Road to an older house in St Leonard's Road at the Hythe. The house didn't have a bathroom, so we had to wash up as far as possible and then wash down as far as possible, and if we wanted a bath we had to go the public baths in Culver Street. They were smashing big baths and they would have someone in attendance who would fill the bath for you. You didn't have control of the taps and if it was too hot you would shout out, 'A bit of cold mate', and you'd say what number you were in and he'd go along and the water would come through either hot or cold. And you would hear lots of singing going on because everybody sang in the bath. It was quite fun really and they were open Sunday mornings as well, so that was a nice little outing really. I think that we had to pay 7p a time.

Jim Lawrence (born 1933)

Our Coal Place Was in the Kitchen

I was brought up in a council house in Wick Road, Old Heath, which was built in 1932. When you came in the front door, there was just a very small hall, which went directly upstairs. At the front downstairs was the living room and the kitchen led off from it. In those days, you had the coal place where they used to shoot all the coal inside the kitchen. All the council houses on that estate had their coal places indoors. Leading off the kitchen was the bathroom with a copper and fire underneath. There was no washbasin and you had to ladle the water out of the copper into the bath. And when you did the ironing you had to plug the lead into the electric light socket.

Joy Cardy (born 1934)

We Used to Store Between 50 and 100 Bicycles in Our Back Garden

I grew up at No. 148 Layer Road, which was not far from Colchester United's football ground. On match days, many of the supporters would ride in on their bicycles and, like many other houses in the road, we would open our garden and charge a small amount to store their bicycles while they were at the match. And that was how I earned my pocket money. We would charge sixpence a time to allow them to leave their bikes in the garden, or 1s if they preferred to leave them under cover in the garage. And because we had a fairly large garden, we could take in between 50 and 100 cycles which, of course, earned me a good little profit.

David Judge (born 1938)

We Had to Scrape the Ice Off the Inside of Our Windows

Dividing the front room and the living room was a staircase leading to the two middle bedrooms, on either side. The room on the right had a small fireplace, and was used by mum and dad. When either me or my brother were ill, mum used to tuck us up in her bed during the day and light the fire to keep us warm. We had no other heating upstairs and many a time we had to scrape the ice off the inside of our bedroom windows. I can remember looking at the pretty patterns that the ice would make. Mum used to call them Jack Frost's paintings.

Jacki Barber (born 1941)

My Father Had to Sell His Piano

My father, Archie Fisher, was an engineer and fitter at Brackett's at the Hythe. In the 1930s, just after he had got married, he was made redundant because there was a slump at the time and he was out of work for some time. He was very bitter about it because in order to receive any dole money, they came round and looked at his house and made him sell his piano, which was upsetting for him as he was quite musical. My uncle on my father's side was known as 'Handy', after his own father. He was the first pupil from Old Heath School to get a scholarship to the grammar school, and he also got a job at Brackett's when he left school, working in the drawing office. But later, after he had decided to stand for the council, he was forced to move on because he was going to stand for the Labour Party. He was eventually elected onto the council and in 1938 was chosen to be mayor of Colchester. And I can remember being taken on to the balcony of the town hall to watch the carnival, and then both he and my aunt, and all my cousins, walked down to the town hall steps to take the salute or whatever.

Joy Cardy (born 1934)

Layer Road football ground taken shortly before Colchester United moved to their new home at the Western Homes Community Stadium in 2008.

Chapter Two

Schooldays

The Headmaster Called Me a Rank Outsider

I went to Canterbury Road School, and one day the headmaster called me a 'rank outsider' because we had come to Colchester from Saxmundham to live, and I was new at the school. Mr Hodgson was his name and he called me and another girl, Catherine Percy, outsiders because we did not belong to Colchester. He was nasty about it. My class teacher at Canterbury Road was Miss Sutherland and she couldn't do her sums very well. One day, I was the only one who got my sums right and she made me write it all on the blackboard. She said, 'Come on Dorothy Parish, you're the only one who got them right, now write it down on the blackboard and show the others how you did it.' She took us for every lesson: writing, arithmetic, spelling and everything. I once got a prize for my handwriting, and also two medals for good attendance. We also had cookery lessons and I've never forgot the way I was taught to cook, and what we used to make we could take home for about a penny.

Dorothy Lawrence (born 1897)

I Loved Everything About School

I started at Canterbury Road School when I was five. I loved everything about school and I didn't want to leave. My last teacher we had before I left was Miss Vale and I loved her. She was such a sweet person. Even in those days, I was always knitting and crocheting and one day when I was sitting on our front door step doing some knitting, Miss Vale came past and said to me, 'Margaret, you're never idle are you? You are always doing something.' We used to do knitting for some of the men who had gone off to war.

Margaret Golby (born 1901)

We Always Started Off With Prayers

I started at St James' School at the bottom of East Hill when I was five years old. We always started off with prayers and drill – exercising and marching round the classroom. We had cookery lessons at East Ward and laundry at Barrack Street. And I stayed at the same school for all my school years. The teachers were very strict and they would give the children the cane across their hand. We never wore a school uniform as such, just a pinafore. Some of the children were quite poorly dressed and we used to wear boots with buttons all up the sides. You had to do them up with a button hook.

Ivy Green (born 1906)

A typical scene from morning assembly or 'Prayers'. This particular group is from East Ward School in 1908.

I Was Glad to Leave School

At East Ward School there was a teacher called Miss Seaborn, a funny old girl, but she was very clever. She looked a bit like a man and had her hair done like one. One day when we were at school she said, 'Does anybody know Twinkle Twinkle Little Star?' I said, 'I do, Miss.' So when I came out to sing it – whether it was nerves or not – I couldn't think of the words. Well she got hold of me and she clipped my ear and put me out in the hall, and there I had to stay. I said to her, 'I'll tell my mother when I get home.' When I got married and had got my own little daughter, we were going over Hythe Bridge on one occasion and we met her. 'Elsie,' she said, 'didn't we have a lovely time at school?' I was about twenty-six then and I said, 'I don't remember them, no I don't, I was glad to leave.' I left school on the day I was fourteen and I can remember running up the road.

Elsie Seaborne (born 1908)

I Did All My Education in One Place

I was born at No. 59 Canterbury Road and started at Canterbury Road School when I was five or six years old. I never went to any other school and did all my education in one place. The headmaster was Mr Hodgson and some of the teachers were Mr Fretwell, Mr Soar, Miss Johnson and Miss Vale who looked after the girls. We were taught arithmetic, writing and spelling. I can always remember one spelling lesson. I was in a class and Mr Hodgson, the headmaster, came in and he said to the class, 'Can you pronounce this word?' And I've always wanted to say it – it was 'apathy' – and nobody could say it. And do you know I was saying it correctly to myself, but I never had the nerve to say it out loud. When school started, every day we were all marched in from the playground to the hall where we had singing and prayers. The headmaster's desk was in the hall and he had a place at the side of his desk where he put naughty children. After prayers, we all went to our classrooms where we would stay all day long. The one teacher taught us everything. The teachers were very strict and you had to do as you were told. If you misbehaved, Mr Hodgson would give you the cane – I had it once.

Doris Lawson (born 1908)

I Was Always Getting the Cane for Talking

I started at St John's Green's School when I was five. The headmaster was Mr Cheese and he was very strict. I was always getting the cane for talking. If there was ever anybody talking, it was always me who got the cane – it didn't matter whether it was me or not. On one occasion, after our teacher had given me the cane, I was told to stand outside the classroom. And when the headmaster saw me he took me and gave me another one across my hand. It was a pretty bad one but I never told anyone when I got home. But someone told my aunt what had happened, because my hand was quite swollen up, and I remember that she was quite upset about it.

Doris Thimblethorpe (born 1903)

You Would Be Sent to Stand in a Little Square

I would often get the cane across the hand for misbehaving. It was always the cane or a little stick, nothing else. If ever you misbehaved you would be sent to stand in a little square, which was in the assembly hall next to the headmaster's desk. We would have to stand there and wait for him. And wherever he was around the school, he would come back and say, 'What's the matter with you?', and 'Why are you here?' He would then tell you to put your hand out and would cane you – whack, whack, whack – and then say, 'Go on, back to your classroom.'

John Conner (born 1913)

Former Canterbury Road School pupil Doris Lawson, pictured in 2003.

I Was Horror-Struck on the First Morning

When I moved down here from London in 1920, I went to the local school in Rowhedge. Immediately I got to the school I was horror-struck on the first morning to find that it was co-educational. Children in London were taught to be self-reliant at the age of eight years. At that age the children are split into 'big boys' and 'big girls', and never the twain shall meet. London boys would be horrified to get anywhere near a girl – that would have been real sissy stuff. So when I came here and found that I was expected to sit in a class with girls, my spirits went to zero. But I soon got to like it. When Friday afternoon came we had lessons until we went outside for playtime. When we came back inside much to my surprise instead of going back to our usual classroom, we all assembled in a larger room. All the desks were pulled away and we started a round of country dancing – boys and girls together – and I thought, 'My God, what have I let myself in for?' I slunk away into a corner and the headmaster said, 'Hey you, get in among them, you'll soon pick it up.' I suffered agonies that afternoon. I thought, 'My God, if those in London could see me now, they would laugh their heads off!'

Albert Cork (born 1911)

I Cried My Eyes Out on the First Day

I started school when I was about four. I went to a private school, which was over Watt's Dairy in Military Road and it cost a penny a week. And I remember that I cried my eyes out on the first day. The classroom was just bare boards and hard seats. We didn't do any paperwork, just games really. I then went to Kendall Road School.

Dick Thorogood (born 1911)

We Were Taught to Make a Batter Pudding

We used to have to go to East Ward School for cookery lessons on Monday mornings. We were taught how to make a batter pudding, or how to cook a joint. On one occasion, the teacher asked me and another girl to go to a shop at Scheregate Steps and get a rabbit for our cookery class and, of course, it still had the skin and

Albert Cork, aged eighty-two.

everything on it. Well the teacher didn't know how to do anything with it. At home we used to have a rabbit nearly every week and I used to watch my uncle skin them. So I ended up having to skin this rabbit for the teacher and cut it up.

Doris Thimblethorpe (born 1903)

He Laid Him Over the Desk and Gave Him Six of the Best
I started in the infants at Canterbury Road School when I was five years old. The main boys' school was on one side, in Claudius Road, the infants were in the middle, and the girls' side was round the corner in Barrington Road. Mr Cheeseman was the headmaster upstairs and he always carried a little cane. I remember one boy, by the name of Banks, who was a little terror and was always in trouble. And on one occasion he was playing up and Miss Johnson, our teacher, got Mr Cheeseman to come into the classroom to see him. And I can remember him coming into the classroom with his cane and tipping the slates out that were propped up in the front of the desks, and getting hold of this boy by the scuff of his neck and laying him over the desk before giving him six of the best across his backside. I can always remember that. He did it in front of everybody in the class.

John Conner (born 1913)

Shut Up, You're Breaking My Train of Thought
My favourite lesson was arithmetic and our headmaster at Rowhedge was one of the best teachers I ever came across. Over and again, if we had a lesson with him of any kind he would say, 'We have a little time to spare, what would be the cost of 143 articles at two and three farthings each?', and we would have to try and work out in our heads that sort of problem. I remember one day in particular he said, 'Let's see if we can do this one in our heads.' I remember saying, after a little while, 'A guinea.' He said, 'Shut up, shut up, you're breaking my train of thought.' Then after about ten seconds he said, 'What did you say it was?' I said, 'A guinea.' He said, 'That's right. You beat me hollow that time, which way did you do it?'

Albert Cork (born 1911)

John Conner, aged ninety, in 2003.

This class from Canterbury Road school in 1913 contains sixty pupils! Note also the tiered rows of desks rising towards the back of the class, allowing the teacher a clear view of everyone in the room.

We Used to Play Leapfrog and High Cockalorum

Our desks were all set in lines facing the front, and there were steps going up to the back of the class. The desks were all grouped in twos, with perhaps between forty and forty-eight children in a class. In front of each desk was a little slot with your slate in, and every child had one. It wasn't just for the younger children, but for all ages. You would use this to write and draw on and then you would rub it off. Once a week we would go to St John's Green School for woodwork or domestic science. I remember making a bronze ashtray. I had to cut it all out and then knock it into shape. It looked quite nice at the finish and I had to buy that for 'tuppence' or 'thruppence' (two or three pence). At playtime, we would play games such as leapfrog or high cockalorum. This is where one boy would bend down against a wall and someone else would then jump on his back, and then he would get off and bend down behind the first boy. And then someone else would try to jump onto both of them and then he would join the other two and so on.

John Conner (born 1913)

We Had to Lay Down and Go to Sleep for a While

I started school in the infants class at Old Heath when I was four of five years old. There must have been forty or more in the class, and after lunch there was a compulsory rest time when everybody had to lay down and go to sleep for a while. I left Old Heath in 1943 when I was eleven years old. I then went to Colchester Grammar School after passing my 11 Plus. It was a much bigger school, which made it a little daunting at first. It was a well-equipped place with lots of new children to form relationships with. The head teacher at the time was Mr Fletcher, but most of the teachers were away at war so there was a lot of temporary staff employed. I particularly enjoyed science- and physics-related subjects.

Hugh Harvey (born 1932)

Joy Cardy, aged five, in 1939.

He Threatened to Give Me a Good Hiding

When we moved to the Hythe I went to Canterbury Road School. I used to walk there across the allotments and the recreation ground, there and back, twice a day because I used to go home for dinner. It was a long walk. When I first went there was a boy called Robert, who was the best fighter in the school, and he threatened to give me a good hiding in the playground. Well I didn't think that I was much of a fighter, and I remember one day standing in the playground and I decided to go up to him to see whether he was going to give me a good hiding or not, and when I tapped him on the shoulder and he turned round. It turned out that he was more frightened of me than I was of him so we never did have our fight.

Jim Lawrence (born 1933)

We Used Sand Trays to Write Our Letters

I started at Old Heath School in 1938 when I was four years old. In the first class we used to have sand trays to write our letters in. There was a big fireplace in the room, and in the winter they would have the fire alight and we would sit in front of this fire and have stories read. It was also useful for warming the milk when it was very cold. I can also remember that we had little mats that we would rest on in the afternoon. Mr Hindle was the headmaster and there was one class for each year group. I remember that you could buy different types of biscuits for a ha'penny at lunch time, and a bottle of milk. You could either have pasteurised or unpasteurised and you would drink it through a straw.

Joy Cardy (born 1934)

My Father Promised Me a Piano If I Passed My 11-Plus

I started at St John's Green School when I was five years old. I really enjoyed my time there until I was eleven and took the 11-Plus to go to the high school. I remember that my father promised me a piano if I passed, and when I did actually pass the exam, I think that the poor man was quite shocked. He didn't expect his daughter to pass that and I found out some time later that he had emptied his bank account to buy that piano, and I've been grateful ever since for that. The girls' high school in those days was split into two buildings. The Grey Friars building housed years one and two, and the years up to sixth form were housed in a building on North Hill, where the current Sixth Form College is located. This was an entirely

Left: Joan Watson, aged six, in 1940.

Below: A class group from Old Heath School, *c.* 1950. Jill Thorogood can be seen in the third row from the front and fourth from the left.

different school to St John's Green, because we had different subject teachers rather than being taught nearly everything by the same teacher.

Joan Watson (born 1934)

We Attended St Peter's Church for Morning Assembly

I first went to Old Heath School when I was about five years old. I can remember that it was mainly play, rather than lessons, at first. We had a large Wendy house in the corner of the room and we had some sand that we played with. And every afternoon we had to lie down for an hour on the floor on these dark red blankets. We had to have a sleep. When I passed the 11 Plus examination, I moved to what was then the North East Essex Technical College on North Hill, later known as the Gilberd. There was only one other person from Old Heath who came with me, and this was a boy named Keith who lived in Whitehall Road. The Gilberd School was very different from what I'd been used to at Old Heath. The work was much harder and it seemed to me that most of the pupils were much farther advanced than I was. We had physics and biology, which we hadn't done at Old Heath. And we also started learning French, which was something that I'd never done before. Our headmistress was Miss Twyman, who was very nice, but did look severe. She was very much a disciplinarian, but always very nice when she spoke to you. Two or three times a week we would all be marched across the road into St Peter's church for school assembly. We would gather together on the school drive and then the teachers would hold up the traffic on North Hill while we all surged across. It took some time for us all to cross the road and I'm not sure that they would be allowed to hold up the traffic like that now. This was the whole school – hundreds of pupils. When we arrived in the church, Mr Sprason, the headmaster, and Miss Twyman officiated at assembly. At that time we didn't have our own assembly hall in the school.

Jill Thorogood (born 1943)

This group photograph shows the senior forms and teachers at the Gilberd School around 1958. Miss Twyman is seated in the centre of the front row next to Mr Sprason, the headmaster.

It Was Understood There Would Be No Talking in Church

Twice a week we took morning assembly in St Peter's church. Going to church was an experience for many of the children, the majority of whom had never been to church. When we went in there, the children had to maintain absolute silence. I would be standing at the front and they would all go and settle in the pews, and it was understood that there would be no talking. I even made sure that staff members didn't disturb them in any way at all. The children were all going to have at least 5 minutes hush. And as time went on we would have over 950 children, plus about sixty staff in attendance. The assembly lasted for about 20 minutes and then the children would all file out of church and wait to cross the road back into school. This was done in stages as the teachers would stop the traffic to allow them to cross.

Alice Twyman (born 1906)

She Threw the Hammer at Him

The teachers were very much different to what they are today. One of our teachers was a Miss S—, who I think was absolutely horrible, and she used to have a little wooden hammer that she kept on her desk. On one occasion, when a boy wasn't paying attention, she threw this hammer at him, but he saw it coming and ducked and it hit the boy behind. It hit him in the eye but nothing happened about it – he just rubbed his eye and cried for a little while and nothing more was said. I remember on another occasion when we were playing rounders and the ball was flying straight towards me; so I put my hands up – more or less to save myself – and the ball came right through my hands and hit me on the nose, causing it be bleed quite badly. Thankfully, though, the bloke was given out because it qualified as a catch! When I was eleven, I moved to Wilson Marriage School and I can remember that all around the main hall they had these religious writings. One of them said, 'The Fear of God is the Beginning of Knowledge', and I can remember that used to frighten the life out of me.

Jim Lawrence (born 1933)

St Peter's church at the top of North Hill, where pupils from the nearby Gilberd School would attend twice weekly for morning assembly.

Joan Watson, pictured in
December 2013.

Ladies Do Not Eat in the Street

Our headmistress at the high school was Miss King, who was very old fashioned
and a real disciplinarian. She kept order and we would never want to upset her if at
all possible. There was a certain length for what our skirts should be and she would
say, 'Kneel on the floor, ladies.' We were all called ladies, and if your skirt didn't
touch the floor when you knelt down you would be told to get the next size skirt.
On one occasion when we were making our way from the North Hill site to Grey
Friars for a particular lesson, some of us went into a shop to buy what we used to
call a 'penny bun'. And all of a sudden, while we were eating our buns, Miss King
shouted out, 'Ladies, what do you think you are doing? Ladies do not eat in the
street. You will see me outside my study this afternoon.' And from that time to this,
I cannot eat in the street. I really cannot and I fully agree with what she said. But
she was a real character.

Joan Watson (born 1934)

We Were Given a Large Spoonful of Cod Liver Oil

My brother was about four-and-a-half years old when he started school and I was
sent with him, even though I was only three. Mum was expecting another baby,
and with nana to look after as well, they allowed me to join the baby class to help
ease the pressure on her. Each day at school, we all had to line up in the cloakroom
and receive a large spoonful of cod liver oil, which made some of the children gag.
This was followed by a spoonful of malt, which I loved. We all had our own spoon,
which had a small hole bored through the handle, and was threaded with a piece
of string, which hung on a hook with our name on in the cloakroom.

Jacki Barber (born 1941)

Chapter Three

Occupation & Trade

The Horseman Worked by Candlelight

When I left school, I worked on my father's farm and he was very fond of working horses. My father wouldn't let us work on a Sunday and he would feed the stock himself with the food he had got ready the day before, and then he would do the milking. We were always busy. One of the horsemen would get to work at four o'clock in the morning and in the winter he had to work by candlelight. When he started on the horses, it would be time for us to get up ready for the other men who started at five o'clock. They would begin by feeding the horses before getting them ready for work. At that time of day, there used to be what were called 'forage merchants', who would take the hay and straw to London to feed the horses there. The money from that was then used to buy manure. We were not far from the railway and we would cart manure from the railway to our manure heap. Our horses would always be ready for a six o'clock start and then father would always have them brought back at eleven o'clock and put in the stables for feeding and then back out again until three in the afternoon. I worked with horses for most of my working life until the tractors came in. When you are using horses in field work, you have company and they used to become very tame.

Walter Barritt (born 1892)

Walter Barritt, aged 100.

Police Sergeant Harry Salmon in 1925.

They Were Short-Staffed Because of the War

I joined the police force on 7 February 1919. I went into Colchester police station and asked if they had a vacancy for a police constable and, of course, they did have because they were short-staffed because of the war. Chief Inspector Simpson came out from his office and had a chat with me and I was sent round to see Doctor Maybury, the police surgeon, who examined me, after which I returned to the station for a meeting with the Chief Constable, Captain Showers. Then they told me that I could start on Friday night as a fully-fledged constable. So I ended going out on the beat with a man named Rivers, and after spending a while with him, I was given my own beat. Most beats only lasted for an hour and we would have to start off at a quarter past ten, and then be at various checking points along the way at quarter hour intervals. So the sergeant could pick you up anywhere on the beat at any of these checking points every quarter of an hour. If you were not at the checking point, the sergeant would then go back in the direction that you should be coming to see if he could find you. He would know something was wrong if you hadn't turned up.

Harry Salmon (born 1895)

If You Earned a Pound You Were Well Off

When I started at Hollington's clothing factory, a woman called Ethel taught me for a month on how to put patch pockets onto men's jackets. After the month was up, I went on my own and it was all piece work. And when I took my first bundle up for the forewoman to pass it, she said, 'I don't think much of your work.' She didn't think that it was good enough and I had to unpick them all and do it again. On another occasion, when I was about seventeen, I went up to the forewoman and she gave me a bundle of leather jackets and I'd got to put the patch pockets on them. And there was only that bundle to do and she told me what the price would be. And I said to her, 'I'm not going to do them for that price.' So she said, 'You'll have to.' I said, 'I shan't.' She then said that she would go and tell the manager and I said, 'I don't care if you do, I shan't come in this afternoon.' And I didn't go in. When I went in the next day, they were still there, so I thought that I'd better get on with them. And the forewoman came down to me and said that she'd had a word with the manager and that they had agreed to give me a few coppers more for doing them.

29

So I said, 'Well that's not a lot is it?' So she said, 'You're not British.' I said, 'I'm as British as you are.' It was all piece work at Hollington's, and if you earned a pound, you were well off. They used to put your wages in separate little tins with your number on it. And on Friday night we used to have to go up to the bench where the old forewoman stood to get our money. And everyone knew how much you'd got because she would be saying, 'This is yours and there's so and so in it', and if anybody earned a quid (one pound), my giddy aunt, all eyes were upon them.

Margaret Golby (born 1901)

Left: Margaret Golby, former tailoress at Hollington's clothing factory.

Below: One of the work rooms at Hollington's factory in the 1930s.

Above: Harry Loome's High Street drapery store in the early 1900s. The building is currently used to house McDonald's restaurant.

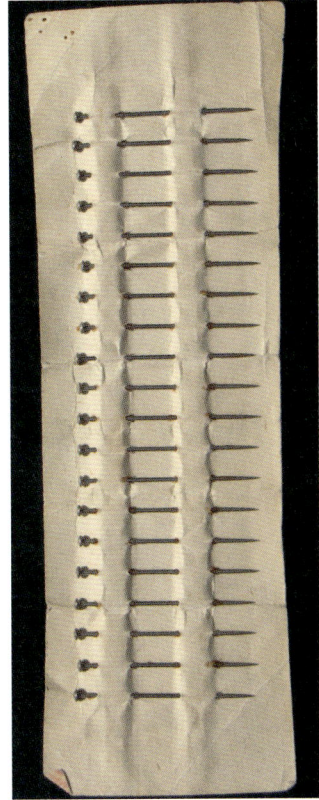

Right: A strip of pins like this was given to customers in lieu of their farthing change.

I Got Paid 2*s* a Week

I started work at Loome's in the High Street when I was fourteen and was paid 2*s* a week to start. I worked from nine in the morning to six at night, and until seven on a Friday and eight on Saturday, although we had a half-day off on Thursday. It was a big drapery shop and Harry Loome, the owner, would come into the shop nearly every day. There were about twenty people working there and I worked on nearly all the different counters, but finished up on corsets and underwear. I also had to get all the orders up for people to collect. The carriers used to bring orders in from the country and I would have to get the orders ready for them to take back. Orders would be for all sorts of things, including cottons, buttons, materials, towels, sheets, wools and children's and baby wear – nearly everything. Some of the assistants lived in and had their own room over the top of the shop. There was no self-service in those days. Everybody had to be served and you were not allowed to say that you hadn't got anything – if they left the shop without anything, they would soon be after you. Mr Piper was a shop walker and would attend to special customers, but he didn't actually serve anyone but would just take orders. He would walk about and if you weren't serving a customer properly, he would tell you to get something else and show them – you had to show customers everything you'd got, you mustn't say that no, you hadn't got it. All of the goods were marked up with prices ending in three farthings. But we didn't give the customers their farthing change, but would give then a packet of pins instead.

Doris Thimblethorpe (born 1903)

I Used to Drive the Bullocks to Colchester Market

I later went to work at Peacock's farm and I used to milk the cows. I used to have to milk eight cows every morning. I worked from 5.30 a.m. until 5 p.m. It used to take me a quarter of an hour to milk each cow. A man used to come from Wivenhoe at a certain time to pick up the milk, so you had to get it done early. We used to strap the legs of the cow sometimes so they couldn't kick out at you or kick the pail over while you were milking. We were never allowed to take any milk home for ourselves – we had to buy it for a penny a pint. We also used to collect the eggs from around the farm and we used to get so much a dozen for picking them up. I remember on one occasion I took some eggs home that I'd picked up and my mother wouldn't accept them – so I had to take them back. After I'd finished milking about eight o'clock, I had other work to do, like feeding the cattle and the sheep. And I'd also got two ponies to look after as well, and some pigs and between twenty and thirty bullocks. We used to have to grind all the food by hand. I also used to have to drive the bullocks to Colchester Market. And on the corner of Maidenburgh Street, there was a shop called Joslins, and the bullocks would sometimes get in there. They used to go in one door and come out the other end. And when we got to the market we used to tell the auctioneer how many bullocks we had brought and they used to give us tuppence. And then we got home we had to go straight back to work again – we never got any time off. We still had to do all our other work.

Ernie Went (born 1905)

I Earned Two and Sixpence a Week

I left school before my fourteenth birthday and my father apprenticed me to a fitter/turner at the Colchester Lathe Company. I worked from six in the morning 'til half past five. I was paid 2s 6d a week, from which they stopped me tuppence for some reason or another. My mother took 2s for my keep and I had the fourpence. I thought I was a gentleman – you could buy a lot for fourpence, you know. I started off at the Lathe by cutting pieces off steel bars with a machine saw. You start off by doing that and then you gradually did drilling and shaping and then from shaping to working on the lathe. Once you can work a lathe, that's the top of it. We weren't allowed to stop for a break. You would keep on working and eat where you stood. You were not allowed to smoke at work, although I did on one occasion and they came out and caught me. They were very strict at the Lathe Company then.

Albert Hewitt (born 1903)

There Used to Be a Lot of Fighting

We had to do point duty at the top of North Hill and at Headgate Corner. When I first started, we would have to stand for four hours at a time before we were relieved, and I remember that on some occasions I would be ready to burst but you had to stay where you were. Eventually, the Chief Constable got to hear about it and he changed it so that the man on the High Street beat would relieve the man on point duty every hour. There used to be quite a lot of fighting in the town on Friday and Saturday nights. This was particularly the case in the High Street and around St Botolph's Corner. In most cases, when a policeman arrived everything would quieten down a bit. In the early days after the war, there was quite a lot of fighting between the hussars and sailors in the High Street, and the blood used to fly then. However, with the help of the military police, we used to get over that quite well. The older policemen used to go to the top of the High Street where there was not too much trouble, but down the bottom of the High Street is where the trouble used to be. And, of course, being full of authority, as you might say, I would often go in and clear the lot up. Sometimes you couldn't see me for blood when I got back to the station. There was no question of assaulting a policeman in those situations. It was give and take.

Harry Salmon (born 1895)

The Trams Would Graze Your Shoulder as They Went By

After I left the Army, I was walking up Colchester High Street one day when I met a friend called 'Strictland', who was in the police force. He told me that there was job going in the force and suggested that I apply. And that's how I came to join the police. I had a writing lesson and a few sums to do, which was not too difficult. I was then interviewed by the Chief Constable, Col. Stockwell, who was a very strict, but good man. There was no nonsense with him. I was sworn in front of a magistrate the following Friday and was given the number twelve. The police station in those days was under the town hall. It was quite a small place with about fifteen policemen in it, and the cells were there as well. My first tour of duty was two weeks on nights. To start with I was with one of the older policemen. We went to the war memorial but did not start our beat for nearly an hour – we just stood there and fiddled about. Then he said, 'We'd better start our beat.' This took us down East Hill, Roman Road, Castle Road and back down East Hill, trying every door all the way down. Then we went over the bridge up as far as the railway crossing. And then we came back to Brook Street, through Childwell Alley as far as the Brook Street railway bridge and then back to the police station. During the day, two men would be on the High Street and two men on Head Street, one hour doing point duty and one hour patrolling. The point duty would be done at the top of North Hill and at Headgate. I wasn't too keen on point duty, as it used to be very cold standing at the top of the hill. The trams would be running up and down and they would graze your shoulder as they went by.

Geoff Bendall (born 1902)

We Never Had Calculators in Those Days

I left school at fourteen and attended night school at East Ward to learn shorthand typing. I also had a part-time job inuPoyser's in the High Street. After that, I got a job at Mendham's, the bookmakers, in St Botolph's Street. I had to help out with the bookkeeping, and we used to have to work out all the bets. They used to employ what they called 'runners', who would go round the town taking bets off people. They would then bring these bets into us. I remember on one occasion one of these runners being given the sack, because he would be bringing these bets in after time, which wasn't allowed because he would be cheating the firm. We had to work out all the winnings in our heads – we never had calculators in those days.

Ivy Green (born 1906)

I Got a Needle Through My Finger

When I left school, I didn't know what I was going to do, but my father managed to arrange a job for me. My father was at his bowls club dinner one day and Mr Crowther, the owner of the local clothing factory, was sitting next to him.

Mr Crowther said that he had lost a stone from his ring so my father got down on the floor and found it for him. So Mr Crowther said, 'Anything you want, just let me know.' So when I left school and was ready for work, Mr Crowther gave me a job at his clothing factory. When I first started I had to take the garments to pieces that had just been tacked together. I had to take the tacking out. Gradually, you got so that you went on a machine. One girl would do the sleeves, another the front and then the pockets. Everything had to be matched. And my first job was making the fronts of the coats before they were joined together. They used to give us a great big bundle of work and you had to wait for your money until you had finished them – it was all piece work. I was working on some big overcoats once and I got a needle through my finger – twice this happened. The first time I did it the needle went through my thumb and I couldn't get it out, so I had to go to hospital. But the second time I just pushed the needle out through my finger, which was very painful. All the girls were very friendly and at Christmas time we would have a lovely party. We used to sing the latest songs while we worked, but I cannot remember what they were now. And we used to go on an outing to Southend in the summer.

Doris Lawson (born 1908)

All the A12 Traffic Came Through the Town

I joined Colchester police force in 1929 when I left the Army. I was interviewed by Col. Stockwell at his headquarters in Culver Street, opposite Pelham's Lane. After completing a written examination, I was accepted and had to go before the Watch Committee and then be sworn in by the magistrates. I was then a Colchester policeman and my number was eighteen. For the first month of duties, you went round with the CID people in order to familiarise yourself with the town and generally introduce yourself to police work. You were not given a new uniform until the time came round for the issue of new ones. I was given the uniform of a policeman who had recently retired. We used to do point duty at the top of North Hill and at Headgate. In decent weather, you would stand for an hour, and then a colleague would relieve you and you would go on patrol. The traffic could be fairly heavy at that time, as all the A12 traffic had to come through the town – the

Bill Geddes, pictured in 1950.

bypass not having been built. We had to do point duty until ten in the evening, although at times this was really unnecessary. It was a cold job in the winter and latterly they gave us some mats to stand on. I have come off duty and not known I had a pair of feet.

Bill Geddes (born 1905)

It Wasn't Hard to Drive a Horse

We used to use a horse and cart to deliver the milk in those days. I arrived at work at half past four in the morning, ready for a five o'clock start. The stableman used to get the horse harnessed up, and then I would put it in the shafts and drive it to the platform to get it filled up, and then away we'd go. My horse's name was Ginger. It wasn't hard to drive a horse, it's only common sense. If you want the horse to go one way, you pull that side of his rein and he goes round. If you want him to go back, you pull his head back. When you want him to go you just touch him and say, 'Go on Ginger.' There used to be a water trough along Lexden Road and my horse wouldn't go past that without stopping for a drop of water. It was difficult to control a horse when we were going home. I remember once coming across Head Street and down towards Osborne Street and I couldn't hold the horse back. I struggled and struggled and it just kept on going. And this policeman stopped me and took my name. When I said, 'What have you taken my name and address for?' He said, 'You came across there without being told.' I said, 'What do you mean? You know the rules, you're supposed to give way to horses, not cars. You get on there and you go back and see if you can stop it.' 'Go on', he said, 'I don't want no more sauce.' I said, 'I'm not being saucy, I just couldn't hold her.'

Albert Hewitt (born 1903)

The old horse drinking trough in Lexden Road, which has since been replaced with a modern plant container.

We Never Got Any Holiday Money

My first job was at Mumford's engineering works. I started in the tool room and was paid 8s a week. There was a Mr Tansley and a Mr Measures working in there, and trying to be polite I used to call them 'Sir'. Mr Tansley would then say, 'If you call me "Sir" I'll box your ears.' When I first started, I used to go to work in shorts and didn't wear long trousers until I was about fifteen. I wore a cap and overalls, and the older men wore bowler hats. In the summer, the firm would close down for a week's holiday, or what was called a week's lockout, but we never got any holiday money. We used to be on piece work and you would save some of this money towards your holiday. We used to get paid on a Saturday, and it was given to us in a tiny little cup with a number on it. We used to have to line up for it at a window and tell them what our number was. We used to make pumps for the Navy. They were huge things called 'triple action pumps', and were built for the big battleships, including the *Hood*, *Nelson* and *Rodney*. When the owner Billy Mumford died, the firm was sold to Anderson's in Scotland and we all left. We didn't get any redundancy pay in those days.

Albert Bridges (born 1908)

The Horses Would Start Kicking, Wanting to be Fed

I left school on the Thursday morning, went to the Co-op in the afternoon, and started work on the Friday morning. I worked as a baker's boy for two years before I got a job in the stables. I started there on nine and tenpence a week, and after a year I got a shilling rise. We had horses everywhere. They were all over the place – Wimpole Road, Winsley Road, the Hythe and some down at Clacton – but when the new stables were built in Wimpole Road they used to keep all the horses

The Co-op stables in Wimpole Road, which provided accommodation for over seventy horses.

together. Except, that is, for the six dairy horses. They had to be out at six o'clock in the morning, which meant that whenever someone arrived to get them ready, and turned all the lights on, it would have disturbed all the other horses and they would then all start kicking wanting to be fed. So they decided to turn the old pastry cook's place into a stable and keep the dairy horses there.

Jim Eves (born 1909)

They Were Honest Old Tramps

There were a lot of tramps around in those days, and the rule was that they had to come to the police station at six o'clock every evening and receive a ticket for entrance to the workhouse for the night. They wouldn't allow them to go in the workhouse if they didn't have a ticket. Emma and Grimes were a couple of local tramps and how they lived I don't know. But they were honest old tramps. They never bothered to come into the station, and preferred to sleep rough all the time. I can remember them as a schoolboy. They would be sitting up on the hill where I used to travel to school. Sometimes they would call at our house and ask for a jug of hot water to make some tea with. She used to carry all their goods, all bundled on her back. Old Teddy Grimes didn't carry anything. He used to like his pipe and they used to say that he was a man of intelligence and was always reading a newspaper. But why they led that life, I don't know.

Harry Salmon (born 1895)

In Those Days There Were Lots of Gang Fights

I joined the borough police force in 1937. Prior to that, I had been in the Army, where I was engaged in all sorts of sports – javelin, shot-putting, boxing and a bit of tug-o-warring. Having done that for a while, I was sent on a boxing course at the army physical training centre at Aldershot. I then fought in the inter-army championships, which I won, together with the garrison championships, which I also won. I boxed as a heavyweight and a couple of times I represented the British Army. After that, my regiment moved to Colchester, where I continued boxing. After one particular fight, I was approached by Inspector Westley, a member of the borough police force, who asked me what my plans were for the future. And to cut a long story short, I was able to buy myself out of the Army for £25 and was sworn in by the magistrates as a constable in the borough force. When I joined in 1937, the force was made up of the Chief Constable, Hugh Stockwell, one chief inspector by the name of Clear, four or five inspectors, about seven sergeants and about thirty-eight constables. I was number thirty-two.

George 'Chalkie' White (born 1914)

I Used to Eat a Loaf of Bread a Day

I used to love working with horses. It took me eight years to gradually work up to it and I used to get on well with the head horseman. Mr Gooch, from Wivenhoe Park, used to ride a Hunter, and it ran away once or twice so we had it on the farm and broke it in to do farm work. We used to put it on the field and make it pull a log. When the horses were young, they used to put the harness on it in the yard so they knew what it felt like. There were three horsemen on the farm and they looked after three horses each. The head horseman used to get there early at 5.30 a.m. and feed the nine horses, and the other two horsemen would get there

Colchester Borough Police Boxing Team, 1937/38. PC George 'Chalkie' White is seated in the front row third from the left. PC Arthur 'Jock' Porter, European Police Heavyweight Champion for that year, is seated in the centre of the front row.

at six. We used to turn the horses out on the field at seven o'clock and work them until eleven, when we had our 'bait' (mid-morning break), and then worked on until three o'clock. We then brought the horses back and fed them and then went home and had our own dinner between three and four. We then went back at four o'clock and cleaned them and bedded then down and left off at five. For my elevenses (break), I would have some bread and cheese or meat. Some of the men would have the top of a loaf, cut a hole in it, put a piece of butter in it, have a lump of cheese or an onion, and eat it with a 'shut knife'. I used to eat a loaf of bread a day when I was at work.

Ernie Went (born 1905)

These Orders Have Got to be Delivered

My first job on leaving school was as an errand boy at a grocer's shop called Sach's in the High Street. My hours were from eight in the morning until six at night, although that didn't mean that I was finished because I then had to do various cleaning tasks when the doors were shut. And for this I was paid 7s a week. One Thursday dinner time when I was getting ready to leave off because it was half day closing, the boss told me that I had to deliver a load more orders in Maldon Road, and my cart had been piled up high. So I said that it was my half day today, but he just said, 'John, these orders have got to be delivered.' So I wheeled the barrow up as far as Wright's restaurant in the High Street, put the barrow down, got on my bike and went home. When I went in the next morning, I found out that his son had to deliver all the goods in his old Trojan car. I kept this up for two years and my father said that I needed to have a rise. So he went in to see Mr Sach, who said that he couldn't afford to pay me anymore, so my father said, 'Well he's leaving then,' So I went straight round to Hyam's clothing factory and got a job for fourteen bob a week.

John Conner (born 1913)

Jobs Were Hard to Come By

When I left school in 1924, jobs were hard to come by. For boys it was a chance to learn a trade or become an errand boy, while girls would go into service or get a job in one of the clothing factories. I eventually got a job at an upholstery and cabinet-making firm, where I started on 5s a week, rising to 10s in the second year, 15s in the third year and so on until I was earning a pound a week after five years. The only form of heating in the workshop was a small gas fire and the lighting was also by gas. The sewing machine, lathe, carding machine and the grindstone were all without power and to be operated by hand. My first job on a Monday morning would be to look through a slit in the open door to watch for the arrival of our two employers. First in sight would be the son of the owner on his bike, and I would shout out, 'Five eight.' A few seconds later, on foot, would appear his father and I would shout out, 'Full inch.' On the coded messages being given, extra sewing, hammering and other forms of activity could be heard. Every August, our firm provided an outing to Yarmouth and we travelled there by train in a special coach. Crates of beer were put aboard and were all gone by the time we got there. At Yarmouth we would all split up, with the men going to the pub and the boys on the pier. At lunch time, we would all meet up for a meal in a restaurant and then spend the afternoon going round the shops, often to get out of the rain. On the journey home, some were drunk, most were asleep, and all fed up.

Les Beagen (born 1910)

There Were Lots of Gang Fights

In those days there were lots of gang fights. Gangs of about ten youths would fight each other. There would be the North Gang, the South Gang and the Hythe Gang, etc. I remember the first one I attended. I had been sent to St Botolph's Corner where there was a fight going on, and on my way there I met Jock Willsmore, an older policeman, who asked me where I was going. I told him I was off to sort something out on his patch. He said that he'd better come with me, so I started off at a brisk pace and he said, 'Hang on, there's no hurry.' When we got there they were really going for it – blood all over the place – and there was quite a crowd looking on. When I went in to intervene, he called me back and said, 'Let them carry on for a bit, let them get tired, then we'll sort them out.' He was a wise man, was old Jock – I learned a lot from him.

George 'Chalkie' White (born 1914)

He Ended Up Knocking Them Both Out

The roughest parts of the town were Magdalen Street and Hythe Hill. And Vineyard Street was also a bit rough at times, with drunkenness and fighting. We never used to hurry to events like that. We would give them time to knock each other about and then we would go in and finish it off. I remember on one occasion when

PC Porter, who was a good boxer, was having some trouble with two Australians. He ended up knocking them both out and dragged them to the police station. Another good boxer was PC Pearson. He had a similar set-to with a sailor. The sailor kept saying that he had been a Navy champion boxer and told Pearson that if he hadn't got his uniform on he would give him a hiding. So Pearson took his tunic off and gave him a thrashing. He later had to go in front of the Chief Constable for that.

Geoff Bendall (born 1902)

They Used to Cut the Cloth With Big Electric Knives

I started off at Hyam's sweeping up and then moved on to trimming in the cutting room, and ended up as a cutter in the bespoke department. They trained me up for that and I learned how to mark out all the materials ready for the cutting with the big electric knives. When the war started in 1939, they stopped all the bespoke work and began to concentrate on bulk work making soldiers' uniforms. And most of the young chaps at this time got laid off. And then in July 1940 they called me up. I went into the RAF and was sent abroad in 1942, first to Durban and then on to Egypt and Libya, and finally to Alamein – we followed the Army up. When I was finally demobbed from the RAF, I came back to Colchester and went to Hyam's to see if I could have my old job back, and Mr Richards, the manager, said to me, 'When would you like to start back?' So I went back into the general cutting room. This involved marking out all the coats and trousers from big bundles of cloth, perhaps twenty pieces thick. They then went to the knifeman, who would cut them all up before they were bundled up

PC Jock Porter in training, with PC Bill Geddes looking on.

and sent into the factory for the girls to machine up. There were about ten men who worked in the cutting room, plus about 400 girls in the factory, although we never mixed with the girls. I ended up doing fifty years with the firm, retiring in 1978.

John Conner (born 1913)

They Knew When it Was Coming Home Time

The drivers would start arriving from six o'clock, although it all depended how far they had to go. We had to have all the horses cleaned and ready for them, including all the harnesses and buckles and brass, and then the drivers would put them in the carts. I used to have about twelve or more men in there doing all these jobs. All the horses knew when it was coming home time and it would be a job to stop them as they were eager to get back to the stables. Every Saturday night we used to give the horses a good feed of hot bran mash, to help keep their systems working, and as soon as they could smell it they would start kicking and banging their feet, wanting to get at it. At the end of October, all the horseshoes had eight small holes drilled into them, where we would screw small studs to help the horses get a grip on the icy roads. I've been there some mornings, when it was particularly icy, and had seventy-two horses waiting to be studded up before they could go out. The drivers would have to take some extra studs with them in their pockets because during the day the studs would quickly wear out and would need replacing.

Jim Eaves (born 1909)

I Used to Ask My Customers for a Bucket of Water

We used to have to take food for the horse wherever we went, in his nosebag. When I had my dinner, he'd have his and also some water to drink. I used to ask my customers for a bucket of water for the horse to drink. I often used to stop in Straight Road, Lexden, and have my sandwiches. Well, of course, the old horse used to go to the toilet there, and this woman who lived nearby used to come out with her bucket and spade and scoop it up for her garden. Well one day she wasn't there and the woman next door took it. Oh dear, I had to laugh, the woman further

Albert Hewitt, aged ninety-three.

up the road told me that they were going 'hammer and tongs' over it. In the winter time, when the roads were icy, we used to have to screw studs into the horse's shoes so they didn't slip on the road. You used to carry the studs in your pocket and all you had to do was to get a spike to clean the thread out on the shoe and then screw them in and tighten them with a spanner. They would only last for a couple of hours and then you had to do it again. They didn't half wear out quickly.

Albert Hewitt (born 1903)

The Horses Used to Know Your Voice
We used to plough an acre a day with a pair of horses. With a double plough, we would do 2 acres. To keep a furrow straight, you had to keep the horses tied back so they all kept level – they'd have tie-backs on them – so they couldn't go too far forward. To get a furrow straight you would put a stick in the ground at the other end, and one in the middle, and you just walked towards it. The horses used to know your voice. If you wanted them to go to the right, we used to say 'woady', and to the left, 'cubby wee'. And if we wanted them to keep straight, we used to say 'height, height'. In the hot weather, the flies used to worry the horses, so we used to put some elder round their neck and a thin bag over their back. Flies don't like elder. At harvest time, we all had to work until eight or nine at night. In the beginning, we never had a combine and had to do it all by hand. We used to cut the sheaves with a binder, pulled by three horses. We used to cut about 15 acres a day. Some of the horses that we used weighed nearly a ton. To stop a horse from running away, you put a running line onto it. You put the plough line right through and tied it on the bit, so when you pulled the horse's head back, it couldn't run away. You can't stop a horse from running away unless you can bend the head back.

Ernie Went (born 1905)

I Took My Tool Bag and Roll of Lino on the Bus
We seldom worked for anyone who didn't have servants. When arriving at a house on one occasion I rang the doorbell, and when the maid opened the door she almost had a fit and screamed, 'The tradesmen's entrance is round the back!' The news of my 'crime' spread like wildfire and by the time I had received a telling off from my boss, I felt that I had rocked the stability of the country. On another occasion, I was sent to fit some lino at a house in the country. I took my tool bag and the roll of lino on the bus and I was finally dropped off in a little lane, only to find that the house was a 3-mile walk away. When I arrived at the house, before I could start, I had to move all the furniture out of the room and clear the floor of tacks. And after struggling to get the cold lino down, all the furniture then had to be put back. When I'd finished the customer said, 'It's the maid's day off so I cannot give you a cup of tea, but here is sixpence.' I then had to walk back to the bus stop and wait half an hour for the bus to arrive, and by this time it was snowing like mad.

Les Beagen (born 1910)

When We Launched a Craft it Was a Great Day
The main ships that we built at Rowhedge were the 'Stern Wheelers'. They were up to 130 feet in length, about 30 feet wide, about 5 feet deep and they would float on a 5-foot draught. Many of the craft that we built were sent to places like

the Sudan and because it wasn't practical to send out a craft complete, once we had assembled a craft and tested it, it would then be dismantled and crated up ready to be reassembled in kit form. We only built the steel hulls here; we never did any of the woodwork or fitting out. We would put the engine on board and line up the shafting and so on to make sure that everything fitted and worked before we dismantled it. You wouldn't be able to sail a vessel to the Sudan. You might get as far as the River Nile, but not much further than that. Once they had been dismantled and crated up, lorries would arrive to collect the crates and transport them to the London Docks. From there, they would be transported out by oceangoing steamers and then by road and railway to their final destinations. On the occasions when we constructed a craft completely, we had to launch it. It was a great day and all the local dignitaries were present, including the mayor, the Corporation and, of course, all the directors and the wives of the firm that we were building for. We would have a big party. Now and again the bottle didn't break. You had to watch to make sure that it did break before the ship went into the water. If the bottle didn't break it was reckoned to be bad luck.

Albert Cork (born 1911)

I Used to Tell the Children the Story about Brer Rabbit

In 1947, I took on the job of Road Safety Officer, which involved going round the schools in the area teaching the children about road safety. This was because there were over a hundred accidents every year affecting children. So I set about trying to reduce it and I got it down to about twenty-five. I used to tell the younger children a story that went something like this: 'Old Brer Rabbit had a lovely bushy tail and every morning he used to go and visit Mrs Rabbit across the road. Before crossing the road he would stop, look right, left and right again and then he would hop across. One day when he was talking to Mrs Rabbit he forgot what time it was and it was getting near lunch. So he says, 'I must be off', and with that he rushes out

The *Nasir*, one of the stern-wheelers built in Rowhedge for the Sudan government in 1929.

and hops straight across the road without looking – and SMACK! A big lorry runs over his lovely bushy tail and this is why rabbits have little tails.' I did this job for eighteen years and was well known as 'Chalkie'. Even now, people often stop me in the street and say that they remember me when they were at school.

George 'Chalkie' White (born 1914)

The Third Hand Was Considered the Lowest Form of Life

I'd made up my mind from very early on that I wanted to work on the barges. Even as a young boy, I was always playing about on the river. So when I left school I had arranged to go straight on the barges. I was going to be employed by the mate at a pound a week, plus my grub. And it so happened that the barge was at Colchester on the day that I left school. So I left school at fifteen, went home and collected my gear, and went straight down to the barge ready to sail the next day. My position as third hand was considered the lowest form of life and you would get all the horrible jobs. After a while, the skipper came forward and stood at the top of the hatchway and threw this little bundle of rag down and said, 'Here you are, get that up because we're sailing first thing in the morning.' And I picked it up and untied the strings and it turned out to be a brand new flag, 6 feet long. And to put that up it meant that I would have to go up to the top of the 90-foot mast. And when I looked up I could see a little old worn out flag, waving away and I thought to myself, 'Cor, I'm not going up there.' And I thought that I would go home. But then I thought, well, if I go home and have to tell my mum that I can't get up a barge's mast, which is going to be my future living, and then I'd got my younger

Road Safety Officer PC George White (*left*) and Sgt Bill Geddes.

brother at home who thinks I'm Superman, so I would have to lose face there. So in the end I was more afraid of not doing it than going up there. It was a test that lots of other people had been given them. As it turned out, and after working well into the night to get it done, because it was dark when I'd finished, and I hadn't had any supper, I managed to get the new flag fixed to the top of the mast.

Jim Lawrence (born 1933)

We Would Fill the Customers' Bottles with Whisky or Brandy

After attending a private business school at Clacton when I was seventeen, I managed to get a job at Wolton and Attwood, wine and spirit merchants, in Colchester High Street. It was located next to the George Hotel and had formerly been owned by the Wicks family. The shop sold all kinds of wine, spirits and beers and we would serve the customers from a row of barrels set behind the counter. And people would bring their own little bottles in and we would sell them a quarter, or perhaps a half-pint measure of whisky or brandy, or anything else that they wanted. I would put the measure into the funnel of the bottle and place it under the tap on the barrel, and then fill it up to the level required. The customers would bring in all sorts of bottles, or perhaps a little brandy flask, or sometimes an old bottle, which could be quite unhygienic and smelly. Sometimes the bottles would smell of fish and the cork would be very old and dirty. We also used to make deliveries to private individuals who had an account with us.

Mary Garner (born 1934)

Fifteen-year-old Jim Lawrence (*above*) and friend Geoff Baker (*below*) climbing up the rigging on a barge.

Left: Mary Garner, pictured in September 2013.

Below: Mary Garner seen behind the counter at Wolton and Attwood's wine and spirits shop around 1954. Note the various wooden barrels containing spirits on the shelf behind.

David Judge, pictured in 2005.

He Stopped Me Sixpence Off My Wages

When I was about twelve or thirteen, I managed to get a Saturday job at Markham's the pawnbroker's in Priory Street. I used to have to put the stock out the front and tidy up the warehouse. Eventually, I was allowed to serve in the shop. On one occasion, old Mr Markham, Hugh Markham's father, came into the shop and said to me, 'We're a bit short today, so I'm going to let you look after the pledges.' This was the pawnbroking side of the business, with its own little entrance round the side of the shop. What fascinated me most in this department was the curious writing machine that we had to use to write out the tickets. It consisted of three old fashioned pens, all coupled together by some contraption, so that you dipped the three different pens into three separate inkwells and then put them across onto three tickets, writing the customer's name and address. On one occasion, this lady came in and wanted to pawn this watch. So what we used to do was to look back to see if she'd had any previous tickets to see what we had advanced her on that occasion, because many people would come in again and again and pawn the same item. So I looked back and saw that about a month before we had lent her 5s (25p) on the same watch. So using this as my guide I did the same on this occasion. And, of course, she was delighted with this and went away happy. When old Mr Markham came back he said, 'How did you get on boy?' So I showed him what I had done and he said, 'Hey, you lent five bob on that gold watch didn't you?' So I said, 'Yes, that's what we lent last time,' 'You never do that', he said. 'You always reduce it. You should have gone down to four and sixpence.' And he stopped me sixpence off my wages at the end of the day.

David Judge (born 1938)

I Had to Sign on the Dole

When the Depression came in the 1930s, there was no work about so I had to sign on the dole. At that time the Borough Engineer, Mr Collins, was able to get a grant from the government to build a new bypass. And they took 300 men at a time who had run out of their unemployment benefit and gave them three months' work at a labourer's wage, under council supervision. Because I was a trained engineer, I managed to get a permanent job there and I used to drive and service the light locos that they used on the railway, which ran alongside where they were building the new road. Willett's had also converted some Ford cars at their garage to run on the railway and they used to travel along there at 30 mph. They were used as a general runabout to take people from one end of the job to another. The road was started at Sheepen and went towards Lexden, and another force started at Greenstead and moved towards the Harwich Road. They had a sandpit there and used to use 7-ton locos to haul the sand via the light railway to build up the embankment for the Ipswich Road railway bridge. After the sand had been piled up, they topped it with clay.

Dick Thorogood (born 1911)

Left: Dick Thorogood, aged about twenty.

Below: The artificial ramp constructed in the 1930s to carry traffic up and over the Ipswich Road rail bridge is still very much in use.

Jim Lawrence pictured in July 2013.

All the Planks Had to be Unloaded on a Man's Shoulder

When we were transporting timber up to the Hythe, all the planks had to be unloaded on a man's shoulder. The dockers in London would load the barge for us, and when we arrived at Colchester there would be a gang waiting to unload us on piece work. They would have one bloke on the stack of timber, four blokes carrying it and another down in the hold to lift the ends up. Each plank was 18 feet long and three by nine in size (3 inches x 9 inches), and it might still have some ice on it, even in June, because it had come from somewhere in the Baltics. And so one bloke would lift the end up, and the next bloke would get it onto his shoulder and away he'd go. While the stack was nice and high it was alright because it was nice and level with the quay. But they didn't just walk on the ground – they made up a little track with the planks, bouncy planks that would be raised up on bolsters, and this would help the men go along. And they would have a similar track coming back empty so they wouldn't bump into the men carrying the planks. When the barge was nearly empty it meant that you got to lift these planks up about 6 feet with this plank on your shoulder. The planks were very heavy but, of course, the men were all toughies. They used to have a special leather shoulder pad to rest the heavy planks on, but you were reckoned to be a sissy if you used one of them.

Jim Lawrence (born 1933)

We Always Had to Look Busy

In 1957, I got a job on a month's trial at Percy King's drapery shop in Crouch Street. My first job was to tidy the counter cupboards and drawers to familiarise myself with the stock, which was all very upmarket. A month later, I was issued with a length of dress material with the instruction to make my uniform, and was given a receipt book in which to write any sales that I made. I very soon learnt that we always had to be (or to look) busy, as Mr Paston constantly walked the shop floor. And at the sound of the shop doorbell, he would step forward to greet each customer individually, and enquire what purchase was wanted. He would then lead them to

Above: In this view of Hythe Quay, dockers can be seen unloading planks of wood from a barge named the *King*. Note the raised planks of wood lying across the quayside for the men to walk on.

Left: Staff at Percy King's shop in Crouch Street pictured on a day trip to West Mersea in the late 1950s. From left: Gwen Wright, Doreen Quinney, Edna Peadon, Jacqueline Carter and Doreen Ifould.

the appropriate counter, calling to the assistant by name. It frightened me to hear, 'Miss Carter, Haberdashery please', especially as he often stood and watched to see how we were serving the customer. Most lunchtimes I would head off home on my bicycle where my mother would have a hot dinner waiting. I'm sure that's how I came to be a fast eater. And as was the custom in those days, the shop was closed on Thursday afternoons. On our afternoon off, several of us 'juniors' would often catch the train to London, which was seven and six return, to go to the larger stores like C&A. We had no shops like that in Colchester at that time and if one girl had saved enough money for a new coat or dress, we all went along to help.

Jacki Barber (born 1941)

Still friends in 2013: former workers at Percy King's.

Percy King's shop in Crouch Street in 1935.

This picture shows the light railway locomotive, which was used for hauling goods and materials during the construction of the new bypass. This view is seen near where the new road cut through the picturesque Lexden Springs, much to the upset of some local residents.

We Saw Another Train Coming Towards Us

On one occasion when working on the bypass at Lexden, I needed to go to Greenstead to get some more diesel. By this time, I was driving a 12-ton road diesel roller. One of the railway runabouts was about to go there so I cadged a lift and off we went at 30 mph. Well along the railway track they had branch lines so that the trains could pass each other, and as we were going along we saw another train coming towards us, so my driver made for the siding. I noticed that the platelayers were working there, but had gone to dinner. He said it didn't matter, so in he went and off we came. He went one way and I went the other. It took him all afternoon to get the vehicle back on the track and I had to walk more than a mile to Greenstead.

Dick Thorogood (born 1911)

We Used to Push Our Way Upriver

When we reached the Hythe, we had to lower our masts before we could get under the four bridges leading up to Marriage's Mill. With a barge full of cargo you needed at least 6 feet of water and you only got that on a spring tide. As soon as we were afloat, we would begin to push our way upriver by using special long poles called setting booms. These were about 28 feet long and were designed so that one end would fit snugly against your shoulder, while the other end would make contact with the bank or the bed of the river. We would often take on a couple of part-timers, usually retired barge skippers, who were called hufflers, to help with this work. It would take about an hour and a half of hard work to push our way up to the mill and the hufflers would be paid 10s each.

Jim Lawrence (born 1933)

The last barge to sail up to Marriage's Mill was the *Raven*, skippered by Jim Lawrence, on 15 April 1984. The barge was to be used as a floating restaurant in conjunction with the then named Colchester Mill Hotel. Other members of the crew on the day were Frank Thompson (seen on the front left side of the barge holding a long pole, or setting boom), and the Greek owner of the Mill Hotel, Emilios Aristodimou, who was anxious to see his barge arrive safely. The man in the small dinghy with the outboard motor is Peter Powell the harbour master. However, things did not go quite to plan and the barge subsequently fell into disrepair before eventually being floated a short distance downriver, where it was broken up and cleared away by Colchester Borough Council.

Most of Our Clients Were Professional People

My first job after leaving school was at Boots and that's where I remained for the rest of my working life. I was there for over thirty years until I took early retirement when I was fifty-one. At that time, the shop was on the corner of High Street and Head Street. I first went on my own for the interview, but subsequently my mother had to come with me so they could get to know her. I was interviewed by Mr Harris, the manager, and I also met Mrs Moon, the head librarian. The library department was on the first floor down at the far end of the shop. The book department, where you could buy books, was on the left, and the library was on the right. The library was owned by Boots themselves and they provided all the books. To subscribe to the library you had to pay a yearly subscription; the Class A subscription got you the very latest books and you had a green ticket, and there was a cheaper Class B subscription, which had older books and that was a red ticket. Most of our clients were professional people who perhaps owned businesses in the town and who were quite well-to-do people generally. My role was library assistant and my job would include dusting some of the books, filing and dealing with customers as they came in, although we didn't actually refer to them as customers, we had to call them subscribers – that was insisted upon. And for some of the subscribers, you had to choose their books for them. You could produce book after book but they would be rejected until finally they might say, 'Yes, I'll give that one a try', much to our relief. My wages were £4 7s 6d a week to start, and we were paid fortnightly in cash. The manager would come round with a tray containing your wages, during opening time, and hand you your wages over the counter, which you would then put into the pocket of your blue nylon overall. It was so incredibly casual. Nowadays, they

This view taken from the brow of North Hill shows Boots the Chemist in its prominent position on the corner of High Street and Head Street in the 1940s. The shop remained in this location until 1970 before relocating to a position further down High Street, and eventually to the Lion Walk Shopping Precinct.

wouldn't dare do that because someone would have seized the tray and be off down the High Street with it.

Jill Thorogood (born 1943)

I Started a Sailmaking Business

When I retired from barging in 1970, I started a sailmaking business in Brightlingsea known as 'James Lawrence Sailmakers'. The barge sails were made of flax, which is a very good quality material and long lasting. In its raw state it is an off-white, fawny colour. The flax came in large rolls 24 inches wide and they were then all stitched together to the shape required. And although some of it could be stitched up on a machine, about a third of the work had to be done by hand. It used to take 147 hours to make a barge mainsail, and that is 1,600 square feet. This would have been based on two men working on the sail. When completed, it would weigh about 9 hundredweight, so it gets heavier and heavier as the work progresses. When the sail was finished, it would be delivered to the crew in its raw state and it was their responsibility to rig the barge. We did everything except for the dressing. A couple of months later when the sail had had a good stretch, it would be taken down and dressed with a solution containing red ochre, which gave the sail its distinctive colour. The work would usually be carried out in a nice clean field where the sail could be laid out, and they would then apply the mixture with a large broom. You could also paint a design or a logo onto the sail at this time as well if you wanted.

Jim Lawrence (born 1933)

54

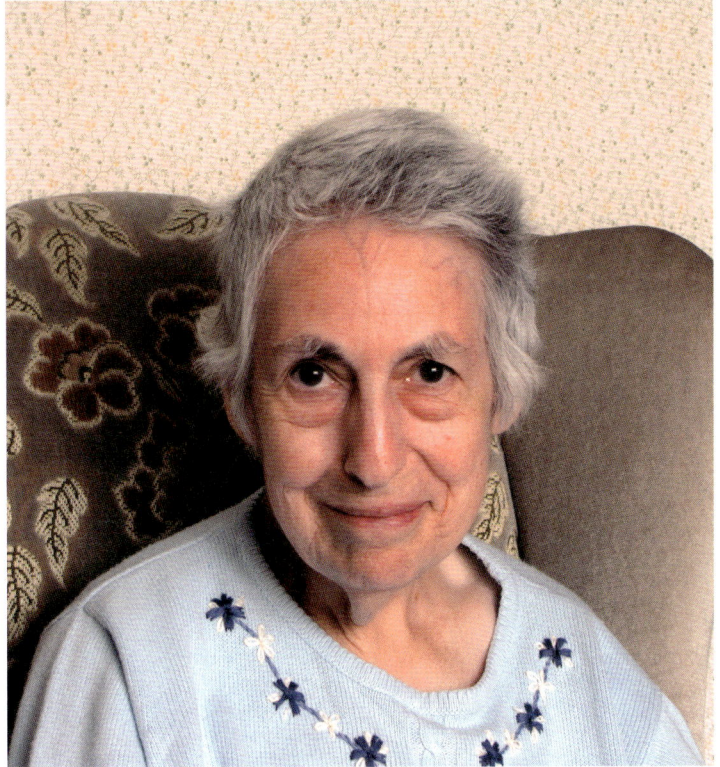

Right: Jill Thorogood, pictured in August 2013.

Below: The people in this picture are carrying the newly completed mainsail for the sailing barge *Kitty*. The sail was manufactured by James Lawrence Sailmakers of Brightlingsea and is now ready to be fitted to the barge. The owner and skipper of the *Kitty*, John Fairbrother, can be seen to the far left of the picture accompanied by other members of the crew.

Chapter Four

Wartime

Shells Were Dropping All Around Us

I first volunteered to join the Army in 1915 but I wasn't needed then. But in 1916, I received my call up papers and went into the Army. I was first sent to Warley where I was equipped with everything a soldier should have, and then I got posted down to Felixstowe for training. After training at Felixstowe, I was sent on an instructor's drill course, and then shortly after I returned from that the sergeant major came up to me and said, 'We would like you to go on a musketry instructor's course, because we are short of instructors.' This was because I had done well with shooting and I was then attached to the Norfolk regiment and went on to qualify as an instructor. So the day came when we were to be sent abroad. We landed at Boulogne and we were all transferred to the Manchester regiment, from where we went to Ypres. I can remember being up to my neck in mud and I never got that mud off me for ages. You had to sleep anywhere you could – it was not very nice, not very nice at all. We eventually found ourselves at Roisel, near St Quinton, and the Germans were giving us hell. Shells were dropping all around us and they broke through on the left and the right of us. They swallowed up nearly all of our division and the orders came through to 'get out as fast as you can', or else we would all have been captured. And as we were retreating we just had to keep going through a barrage of shells; some got through, some didn't. We didn't know where we were for days, but we eventually

Harry Salmon pictured at the time of his 100th birthday.

A soldier stands in a bomb crater in Butt Road following a raid by a German plane in February 1915. Fortunately, the main damage was confined to gardens and outbuildings, and luckily the pram in the garden was empty at the time of the explosion.

got through to Picquigny, which was a little more peaceful. When we got to Dunkirk, everybody had to have a bath before they got on the boat, and some fresh clothing. So we were expecting a nice hot bath, but when the showers came on in the big communal bath, it was like ice. I ended up catching an awful cold and I couldn't speak by the time I got on the boat. I finally got home on 16 January 1919.

Harry Salmon (born 1895)

People Were Going Crazy

I was at school during the First World War and I can remember the time when a bomb dropped in Butt Road. I didn't see it happen, but I remember seeing the damage it caused. There was a pram in the front garden, but luckily the baby wasn't in the pram. I was at work by the time the war finished and I remember that one of the girls was standing on a ladder to reach the top shelves when we heard that the war had ended. She went crazy and I thought that she was going to fall off the ladder. And, of course, we all went out on to the front street, which was quite near to the town hall, to hear them announce that the war was finished. There was lots of cheering and people were going crazy, but we still had to stop at work – they didn't give us the day off.

Doris Thimblethorpe (born 1903)

We Used to Queue a Lot for Food

During the First World War when the air raids came, the siren would go and we would all come out of school and go home. I would have to walk up East Hill, but we didn't have to hurry or anything – nobody seemed to be very frightened. We had no shelters or anything like that in those days. My mother had two soldiers billeted with her during the war. We never had much room, but they used to sleep with us. One was named Coombs and the other was named Taylor, and I can remember as a child going to meet them and they used to bring their guns home, which I thought was thrilling, walking round Castle Road with these guns. All the houses round about had soldiers billeted with them. I can also remember the L33 Zeppelin coming down at Wigborough. My father managed to get a piece of it and had it made into brooches for us. I used to have to queue up as a child to buy butter and meat. We would go to the Co-op in Long Wyre Street for 2 ounces of butter and to Gosling's, or perhaps Cade's, the pork butcher, for our meat. And sometimes you might go past the Maypole and see another queue and you would join that and get another 2 ounces of butter. We used to queue a lot for food during the war.

Ivy Green (born 1906)

The Soldiers Were All Singing and Whistling

I was six years old when the First World War started. There were soldiers galore in the town, and everyone had a soldier or two billeted with them. It didn't matter how many children you had, you still had to take a soldier. We had two staying with us, and they had to sleep on the floor on a mattress. When they were embarking for France, there were thousands of soldiers coming out of the barracks. Officers on horseback and these soldiers all singing and whistling as they went along, and the people lined the streets giving them bread, cakes, fruit and cigarettes as they went by. We used to have to queue up for potatoes and margarine at Macklin and Ranson's. We would stand there for hours sometimes. Then sometimes they would say that they had run out, but we still used to wait until the next lot came in. There was a lot of pushing and shoving. I remember that my older brother used to queue up at the Maypole in Long Wyre Street and he used to carry a box on the back of his bicycle to put his rations in. And one night he lost his bike with his rations in.

Albert Bridges (born 1908)

Queuing in Colchester for potatoes in 1917. The policemen in attendance would have ensured that there was no pushing and shoving or queue-jumping.

This scene from the First World War period shows soldiers marching at St Botolph's Corner, at the foot of Mersea Road, en route to the barracks. Note the open-top double-decker Mersea bus waiting at the junction of Stanwell Street, with either the driver or conductor standing on the bonnet.

Some of the Children Used to Stand and Cry

I was at school during the First World War and when the siren went some of the children used to stand and cry. We just sat in the classroom because there were no air raid shelters. I can remember there being lots of soldiers in the town and they used to form up outside our house. They used to be billeted in people's houses and we had two with us.

Doris Lawson (born 1908)

This Country is Now at War with Germany

I can remember the Prime Minister, Neville Chamberlain, coming on the radio about eleven o'clock on Sunday 3 September 1939 to announce that 'this country is now at war with Germany'. As I sat with my parents, my grown-up brother and sister, and one of my uncles in the kitchen of our house, I had no idea, at nine years old, what it all meant. When bedtime came that day I found that my parents had moved my bed into their room. My mother experienced air raids in London in the First World War, and anticipated the worst. During the first few weeks of the war, families had been evacuated from the East End of London into Essex, and we had a mother and her little boy billeted with us. They were very bored in the country and only stayed about two weeks, which was probably just as well for my father's blood pressure, as the first thing that the little boy had done after arriving was to pull every head from every flower in the garden, which was my father's pride and joy.

Olive Hazel (born 1930)

Olive Hazel, pictured in 1945, aged fifteen.

We Were Both Tearful

When war was declared in 1939, my mother and I were in the dining room listening to Chamberlain on the radio. I think we were both tearful and my father came in and said, 'Come on, there are things to do, we have got to get the cellar ready.' I said, 'I'm not going down into that cellar.' He said, 'We'll put the deck chairs down there and a bit of carpet,' He had got a big shovel and a big broom handle and I said, 'What are you going to do with that?' He said, 'Put this shovel on the broom handle and you come behind me in case we get any incendiaries.' I said, 'Daddy, I'm frightened of fire, are you going to let me do it alone?' He said, 'Oh no.' Little did I know then that within six months he would be dead and I would be doing it alone.

Nora Frost (born 1919)

We Were Fearful of Blitzkrieg Type Air Raids

I remember during the months leading up to the start of war in 1939 that some air raid shelters were being constructed around various administrative buildings, and that air raid sirens were being installed. During the long summer holiday of 1938, I went with the Grammar School Scout Troop (3rd Colchester) to my first scout camp at Braxted Park, just a couple of miles to the south of Kelvedon. We cycled there and back in patrols along the London Road (A12). At that time, the only stretch of dual carriageway was between Marks Tey and Kelvedon and one carriageway of it had been closed and was being used to store military equipment. In a field adjacent to our campsite was a searchlight unit, which we were allowed to visit on occasions and operate the searchlight. When the announcement of the declaration of war was broadcast on the radio, all the family were in our sitting room. It created a feeling of foreboding and fear of the possibility of the Blitzkrieg type air raids we had heard about. It was not many days afterwards that the sirens sounded and we wondered what we should do. It was decided that the safest place for us would under the dining room table.

Tony Blaxill (born 1927)

Tony Blaxill, aged about eighteen, towards the end of the war.

He Saw Me and Let Go With His Machine Gun

If there was an air raid on I used to get my wife in the pantry under the stairs, and I remember one occasion when one of these doodlebugs came over, which was being chased by a Spitfire, and these bullets and cannon shells were rattling down in the road. My wife dived into the pantry only to have all the pots and pans in there falling down on top of her. And I remember being down at Paxman's one day when there was a raid on and they used to make us stop work and go down the shelter. Anyway, I decided that I would go for a walk around the field to get some fresh air – I didn't like being stuck inside – and this Jerry plane came along and dived down towards me. He was no more than 150 feet up and was probably photographing Paxman's. So I dived under this boiler, but he saw me and let go with his machine gun and he hit that boiler and these bullets were rattling on the boiler with me inside. I can hear it now. On another occasion, when I was off duty from the Home Guard, my wife and I were coming up North Hill and there was a raid on. The rockets were all firing on the Abbey Field, as well as other guns elsewhere, and you could hear these planes going over on the way to London. And there was all these bangs going off and we got down as far as Osborne Street and decided to go into the shelter. And there was this bloke in there that was shaking like a leaf. So I said, 'What's the matter mate?' So he said, 'There's an air raid on.' And I said, 'You'll soon get used to it, you don't want to worry about them. If your name's on one of them they'll have you.'

Dick Thorogood (born 1911)

We Had Such Fun With Our Boats in the Water

One of the highlights of my time in Colchester during the war was visiting the American airbase at Boxted. The Americans were so generous with their comics,

Gordon Williams, pictured around 1942 during one of his stays in Colchester.

candy, chocolate and ice cream, which we could only dream about. Our greatest prize, however, was to obtain the disused auxiliary fuel tanks that fixed under the wings and enabled the fighter aircraft to fly into Germany to escort the bombers. They came in two types, cylindrical and oval, the latter being the most prized. The biggest problem was getting them to the water. There were three of us with only two bikes and a makeshift trolley cobbled together from an old pram chassis. Our destination was the River Colne at the Seven Arches, which was quite a long trek from Boxted. We had such fun with our little boats in the water, oblivious to the occasional ducking and the long walk home to Winchester Road.

Gordon Williams (born 1931)

We Hurriedly Put On Our Gas Masks
We used to own a beach hut on the cliffs at Walton, which we used to use at weekends and during the summer holidays. Unfortunately, when war began, we were forbidden to use it and eventually all the huts had to be removed from their positions on the promenade and cliffs. Our hut, along with others, was removed by Mr Oxley, a local Walton builder, and stood in a field for the next five years. It was finally returned to the promenade in 1946, but because the cliffs had been mined no huts were sited on them until 1963. As a family our first taste of action came during the night of 3/4 September 1939, when the air raid siren sounded. It sounded very loud, being only a short distance away from our house, and although it turned out to be a false alarm, we didn't know that at the time and mum and I hurriedly put on our gas masks, thinking that was what we should do, and made for the shelter. Dad soon told us that putting on our masks was not necessary until we heard the hand rattles signifying a gas attack.

David Snow (born 1930)

Every Child Was Issued With a Gas Mask
I can remember the day that war was declared. I was out with my parents collecting blackberries, and a man came along and said to my father, 'It's started you know', and I can remember them being alarmed about it, but it didn't mean a lot to me at the time. I was seven years old when war began and at school we had to spend quite a bit of our time practising what to do in the event of an air raid,

and spending time learning how to put our gas masks on. Every child was issued with a gas mask. Once the underground shelters had been built, we used to have to practise going into them. We had to form an orderly line and then be marched across the playground. I remember them being quite dark inside and we were all jammed together sitting on benches running along both sides of the shelter. The teachers tried to entertain us and sometimes the children would put on little shows themselves. I did one once myself. I had a little thing called 'cinematography' that I had got as a present, with a couple of little films. It was a battery-driven thing, which showed the pictures onto a little screen. I remember doing that.

Hugh Harvey (born 1932)

We Would Sit in the Little Cupboard Under the Stairs

Whenever there was an air raid on, my mum, brother and me would sit in the little cupboard under the stairs, and for added protection mum used to pull the dining room table over the door. I can remember her crawling out from under the table one night to move a small oil lamp from off the old Singer sewing machine and placing it under the table to give us a glimmer of light in the cupboard. At school, no matter how old you were, we all had to do air raid training. This consisted of running around the playground, and when the teacher blew a whistle we had to dive to the ground and lay as flat as possible, presumably so we wouldn't make very good targets. If the air raid siren went off for real, we were marched into a large shelter in the playground. The children were led class-by-class right down to the end of what seemed like a long, dark tunnel. There were wooden benches running down both sides, and a shelf above with hooks on to hang our coats. The children would often sing, 'Ten green bottles hanging on the wall', and I can remember looking up at the shelf for those green bottles wondering why I couldn't see them. On one occasion early in the war, when my mum was taking my brother and I to visit our grandparents, a stray plane decided to have a bit of fun by spraying the streets with gunfire. A man up a ladder in a nearby street was killed cleaning his windows, and the road was jumping with bullets.

Jacki Barber (born 1941)

We Used to Practise Getting Under Our Desks

When war began, I can remember going along to Old Heath School to be issued with a gas mask. My brother was in one of those that completely covered him. We had boxes to carry them in with a string round our necks. Before they built the shelters in the school playground, we had practices getting under our desks in case of an air raid. Later on in the war, we would all go into the shelter when there was a raid on. We had very long benches to sit on and we used to sing songs and have stories told to us, and perhaps there would be a sweet handed round. At the end of the war we had a street party at the junction of Wick Road and Speedwell Road, with tables full of food. There was bunting and everybody provided food and brought their chairs out. Afterwards, we had games and races and that sort of thing.

Joy Cardy (born 1934)

We Had a Shelter Indoors

We had brick air raid shelters built in the playground and when there was a raid on we would all have to go down there with our gas masks. I think that we were

Joy Cardy, a former pupil at Old Heath School.

given our masks at home and that the ARP (Air Raid Precautions) man would come round and tell us how to use them. We had blackout material supplied to black out all our windows. Dad made some frames up and nailed this material on to them. We also had a curtain over the door so that you could go through the curtain, close the curtain behind you, and then open the front door. And, of course, the ARP man would be walking around shouting, 'Put that light out.' They were only ordinary men really, but it gave them a bit of power. We also had a shelter indoors, which they used to call a table shelter. These were provided by the government and they consisted of a great big lump of iron, and my dad had to build it up on the floor. You couldn't have one if you had a wooden floor – you had to have solid floors. It was a huge thing and the whole family could get in there, and you would also use it as a large table during the day. It had a steel top with iron supports and just above the floor it had a spring type metal support for you to put a mattress on. And if there was an air raid on the whole family would get in there. We also had an Anderson shelter in the garden, which we shared with our neighbour.

Jim Lawrence (born 1933)

Put That Light Out

At home we were issued with a Morrison shelter, which was erected in our living room. It was like a huge table really with a sheet iron top, and underneath you could sleep. If your house got bombed, this heavy, steel top might have to withstand bricks and other heavy objects falling onto it. Other than that, there was always a cupboard that you could get into. My father made some blinds with wooden structures and then nailed this black paper onto it, and then every night as dusk approached we had to put them into the windows and shut out every light. This had to be done for every window in the house, if not the air raid warden would come rattling on your door and tell you to 'put that light out'. I can remember when I was about twelve

64

The burnt out shell of Hollington's clothing factory dominates this view of Stanwell Street in February 1944.

years old there being quite a big raid on Colchester. It was around the St Botolph's Street area and the big clothing factory, Hollington's, was totally destroyed. And I can remember going by the following day on the way to school and seeing just the outside wall of the building standing, and it was still smouldering.

Hugh Harvey (born 1932)

The Ground Shook When the Guns Were Firing

In September 1940, having passed the scholarship examination, I became a pupil at the Colchester County High School for Girls in Colchester. It was a lovely September day and we all had to wait in the playground at Grey Friars on East Hill to be told which form we were in and to be met by the formidable headmistress who, after a few preliminary remarks, stated, 'You may have received the mark 'excellent' on your previous school reports, but you will not get that here – no one is excellent at anything.' There were air raid shelters at the school, in the form of enclosed concrete trenches, which had been dug in the flower and vegetable gardens, and over the course of the next few months many hours were spent in them. We entered down a concrete slope and at the far end of the shelter there was a metal ladder leading up to a manhole cover, which was our escape route if needed. Benches ran along either side and we only had a dim light. Although the trenches were almost completely buried, the ground shook whenever the local guns were firing.

Olive Hazel (born 1930)

You Saved Every Bit of Paper You Could

We used to save and collect all sorts of things – matchboxes, newspapers and jam jars. We got to the stage that if you had a cup of tea at the station you were just as likely to drink it out of a jam jar. All those things were so precious. At school the children had so little handwork material. They painted on newspaper and you saved every bit of paper you possible could, backs of envelopes and that sort of thing. They couldn't have a new pencil until the old one was about an inch (25mm) long, they could hardly hold a pencil let alone write with it. By 1940, I was teaching at St Anne's School and we had several air raid shelters on the field

Olive Hazel, a former pupil of the Girls High School in Colchester, pictured in August 2013.

there. All the children had to go in them, although sometimes some children didn't come to school if the siren had gone. In the shelters we sang songs, told stories and played games. The children certainly didn't learn much. There was a channel running down the centre of the shelter with seats at each side. The walls just ran with water and collected in the channel. We had to keep mopping the walls with floor cloths and keep saying to the children, 'Sit up, and don't lean back against the walls.' Their coats got very wet if they leant back. I remember walking from St Anne's School up to the High Street just to get warm, because standing in those shelters for two or three hours you got really cold.

Nora Frost (born 1919)

We Used Old Car Headlights in the Shelter

My father and the Revd Carrick, next door, agreed to share the cost of a concrete air raid shelter at the bottom of Carrick's garden. It was about 8 feet square and had about 6 feet of headroom inside. It was built partially underground with a mound of earth on top. Access was by a concrete stairway on each side covered by horizontal doors at ground level. It had a small oil stove for heating and some seats and bunk beds made up from old packing cases. I also organised some lighting by using our model railway transformer and running two bare copper wires connected to its 20-volt output down to some old car headlights inside the shelter. During the winter of 1940/41, German planes would be flying overhead nearly every night on their way to London. The sirens would sound during the evening and the bombers would drone overhead, one after the other, for several hours on end. It seemed that we were on the flight path of many of these bombers and on one occasion, several bombs came streaming down and exploded in a field at the junction of Braiswick with Bakers Lane, about 300 yards from our house. My mother had been running the bath at the time and she forgot that she had left the taps on as we rushed to the shelter. When we returned to the house, the bath had overflowed and the scullery

Surviving Second World War air-raid shelters at North Primary School in Colchester.

ceiling had been brought down. On another occasion when I was at the grammar school, and in a classroom on the first floor with a good view to the north of the town, we saw a German bomber drop out of cloud cover heading east releasing its bombs over the town, and then disappearing back into the clouds. This was the occasion when the Old Heath Laundry and a nearby house were hit, killing five people. No warning siren had been sounded.

Tony Blaxill (born 1927)

We Saw the Bombs Coming Out of It
Several friends and I were playing in a field behind where we lived at Lexden – I remember that it was during winter and was snowing at the time – and we heard this plane coming. It was a Heinkel bomber and it was flying very low, and we watched it as it went towards the railway line at Chitts Hill. And shortly afterwards we heard this gunfire but we didn't know what it was shooting at. However, we heard later that it had been firing at a train and one of the passengers, who apparently was a pianist, lost all of the fingers on one of his hands. On another occasion, we were out in the playground at St Helena School and we saw this plane come over from the London direction. It was a German bomber, a Dornier perhaps, and we saw these bombs coming out of it, so we dashed like hell to the shelters, and those were the bombs that landed on the Chapel Street area.

Jim Watson (born 1929)

Eighty-four-year-old Jim Watson, who saw bombs falling out of a German plane.

He Just Dropped His Bombs

My big memory of the war is when the Chapel Street area was bombed. We were in school (St John's Green) when we heard this huge explosion and we all got under our desks. And we found out that a German plane was being chased over the town by Spitfires and, to lighten its load so he could pick up speed, he just dropped his bombs willy-nilly, although he wasn't far off from the barracks. It went straight down from South Street, Wellington Street and into Essex Street and all those houses were absolutely devastated. And if it had been just a few feet either way, he would have hit my home, or he would have hit the school. And my mother was at home with my baby brother and she picked him up and ran to the school. There was lots of screaming and other mothers were there thinking that the school had been hit. But that was a very lucky escape.

Joan Watson (1934)

Beds Were Hanging From the Upstairs Rooms

My father, Albert Evans (known as Taffy), was in the Home Guard company at Masons, where he was a timed served engineer and toolmaker. He was aged thirty in 1940 and exempted from military service. He always said that *Dad's Army* was very true to life and he used to go on regular exercises, often at Great Bentley, or further over towards the coast, and they had proper weapons. On one occasion, another platoon member used his gun to vault over some obstacle; however, instead of using the butt end of the rifle, he used the barrel and clogged it with earth. And he very nearly fired the gun without cleaning it, which would have been very dangerous, not least to him, but he was stopped just in time. They also practised with real grenades. Another platoon member removed the pin from a grenade and asked what he should do next. The sergeant seized the grenade and threw it away before it exploded. After the bombings in the South Street area in 1942 the platoon,

Albert Evans (born 1910) was a member of the Home Guard during the Second World War.

which paraded at the Drill Hall in nearby Stanwell Street, was instructed to help with the cleaning up and possible rescue work. They may well have known some of the people who had been killed or injured, but dad said little about that. He did say that there were pet rabbits alive in huts in the garden, and some beds were still hanging from the upstairs rooms and there was rubble and water all around. They had a regular Army sergeant in charge of them and when they had done, he formed them up to march off. However, they were all keen to avoid the large puddles and went round them. The sergeant said, 'This is not what proper soldiers do', and he marched in a straight line through the puddles. However, the largest of these puddles was a bomb crater and the sergeant disappeared from sight!

Albert 'Taffy' Evans (born 1910)

My Mother Was Buried Under the Rubble

On the morning of the raid on the Chapel Street area on 28 September 1942, Mrs Daldry, who lived at No. 3 Essex Street, came round to my mother's house and asked her if she would look after her daughter Gill while she went into town to do her shopping. Having gone off into town, she came back to find that a bomb had been dropped in Essex Street, causing considerable damage to her home, where my mother had been looking after her daughter. The explosion caused the house to collapse and some of the beams fell down from the ceiling above and landed on the mantelpiece, forming a tent, as you might say, and then the rest of the ceiling and other debris came down on top of that. And my mother was buried under all of this rubble cuddling the baby, and the baby kept crying because she was due for a feed. She could hear voices outside and she was shouting, 'I'm here, I'm here.' But, or course, in the initial aftermath of the raid they were running around looking after people in the street who had been injured. Eventually, they dug into the property and worked out that they could get her out by removing the rubble at the front to reach her. After that the house was never rebuilt and, of course, about two weeks later on 13 October I was born.

Dennis Marchant (born 1942)

Dennis Marchant, pictured in September 2013, aged seventy.

We Relied Heavily on Public Transport

As well as the established ARP posts, every householder was asked to place outside his house a bucket of sand, a bucket or two of water and, if possible, to provide a long-handled shovel (a coal shovel fixed to a broom handle) to heap sand from the bucket onto any incendiary bomb to extinguish it. Some people also had stirrup pumps to enable them to pump a jet of water onto a small fire caused by such a bomb. Petrol was strictly rationed for essential users only and so we had to rely heavily on public transport, which was pretty full at peak times and queuing for a bus was common practice. Standing was not permitted on the upper decks, but they allowed up to twelve passengers to stand down below. At night times, to comply with the blackout regulations, the interior lights were cut to a minimum and the conductors would have a cycle lamp fixed to their cash box straps so they could check the fares paid. I remember one occasion when a German bomber shed his load of incendiary bombs on the St Botolph's area, resulting in a massive fire that destroyed several buildings including the large clothing factories. At the time we were at the top of our garden at No. 260 Maldon Road, standing by the shelter, when we saw the huge red glow in the sky over the town and father was concerned about his shop in Head Street. The following day we went down to St John's Green, which was as close as we could get, to view the damage. I particularly remember seeing the main wall of Hollington's factory standing starkly against the other buildings before it was demolished.

David Snow (born 1930)

We All Had to Get Under the Tables

I remember being at school one morning when a bomb fell on Essex Street, at the back of the Playhouse, behind St John's Street. It was a wet morning and the children had gone down to the toilet (they weren't going out to play) and they came rushing back. Some of them said it was guns, and some thought it was a bomb. I said, 'If its bomb, get under the tables.' We all had to get under the tables, and as I was going round tucking them in, the head came in and said, 'Get under your own table, you silly girl.' I said, 'I can't, I've got forty-odd children here getting under their tables.'

And we were saying to the children, 'You are a rabbit, get in your hole', and that sort of thing. We also had to do fire watching duty at North Street School. We had to be on duty between about seven in the evening until the next morning. On one occasion around January time, there had been a lot of shrapnel coming down and we had to stay until it was daylight to make sure that there was none in the playground, because the shrapnel was sharp and the children could have been injured. Even if the siren didn't go off, you were still expected to be patrolling the building for most of the night. In the morning, you went home for some breakfast and then had to be back at school ready for a nine o'clock start. We didn't have any time off. It wasn't quite so bad for the children, who would often drop off to sleep at their tables.

Nora Frost (born 1919)

I Was Sworn to Silence

During the Second World War, Mr Butcher and I had to go to London to the Ministry of Supply. We were told that the government was intending to build something they were calling 'buffer pontoons', which were going to be built in preparation of the invasion fleet. They said that you are running the Wivenhoe Shipyard and you've got the ironworks there to take it on and do it. There was no question of saying no and we listened as this chap explained exactly what these bits were and how they fitted into the scheme of things. It was all terribly secret and he swore me to silence. This, of course, was all part of the Mulberry Harbour. The two structures that we built for the scheme were 80 feet in one direction, 60 feet in another and 12 feet high. They were absolutely honeycombed with steel criss-crossing all the way through the thing, after which we had to fill it with 6 inches of concrete. After we had finished, the deck was as strong as could be. I calculated that each one weighed nearly 1,000 tons and they had to be launched into the river just the same as a ship would be. An Admiralty tug stood by as we launched them and within half an hour we saw the back of them and they were gone. We never saw them again.

Albert Cork (born 1911)

We Were Taken in Small Groups to Find Somewhere to Stay

I can remember being evacuated in September 1940. Most of the children from around here went together. As it turned out, we all went to Stoke-on-Trent, of all places. Other people went to Kettering and some, I believe, to Devon. The whole idea was to get the children away from the east coast. My mother came with me and we had to assemble in the school playground before we were taken down to North station. We were each given a number and we had to carry our gas masks. I think that most of the children were excited because it was like a great adventure. When we arrived there we had to be billeted. We all lined up and a billeting officer came along and we were taken off in small groups to find us somewhere to stay. And I can remember us arriving at this small street, and walking down there, and it was completely different to anything that I'd seen before. Tiny houses altogether with no gardens. Eventually, it was our turn and a woman opened the door in curlers and said, 'Yes.' And the billeting officer said to her, 'This is Mrs Harvey and her son and you'll be looking after them.' And she said, 'Come in.' We didn't get much of a welcome and my mother wasn't very happy about it, but we had to put up with things.

Hugh Harvey (born 1932)

Hugh Harvey, aged nineteen, pictured in his RAF National Service 'best blue' uniform.

We Were Evacuated En Masse

Not long after the outbreak of war, when I was eight years old, I was sent from London to live with my grandmother in Winchester Road. I was enrolled at Canterbury Road School and soon was integrated into a happy school life. I recall that my classmates were kind and friendly, although I was teased about my accent, which could have had a hint of cockney. But this way of life was not to last because in September 1940, we were evacuated en masse to Higham Ferrers in Northants. When we arrived, we were lined up to be picked out like cattle in a market to join our prospective guardians. I had no contact with my family for a year – my father was in the Navy and my mother in war work – and letters were very scarce. It can be summed up as the most miserable period of my life. No counselling or help. You just had to make the best of it.

Gordon Williams (born 1931)

It Began to Machine Gun the Street

We eventually returned to Colchester and on one occasion, following a school visit to the castle, we were walking down Long Wyre Street when the distinctive noise of a German bomber was heard overhead. It began to machine-gun the street and some of us were hastily taken into a butcher's shop and pushed into a large refrigerator at the back of the shop. I'm not sure how long we were in there other than feeling mighty cold and brushing against the hanging carcasses.

Gordon Williams (born 1931)

Wish Me Luck as You Wave Me Goodbye

In September 1940, at St Anne's School, we were suddenly told that we would have to evacuate the children right away. In the afternoon the mothers came to the school and the head teacher, Miss Price, got the children outside and singing, 'Wish Me Luck as You Wave Me Goodbye.' They had all the mothers in tears and then we started going down to East Ward School, where we had to assemble. A bus then took us to the station. We had 300 children and mothers in a non-corridor train and we left

North Station about three o'clock in the afternoon and arrived at Kettering about eleven o'clock at night. We spent the night on the floor of Kettering Grammar School and the next day we were billeted in the villages. The people were there to meet us off the bus and I remember one particular woman coming up to me and saying, 'Are you a teacher, do you want a billet?' She didn't want any children so I was welcomed with open arms. We had to go to the local school and join in with them. I think there were four Colchester teachers in the school that I was in and I'm not sure how many children. The children started wanting to go back home when the expected invasion hadn't take place, and within a few weeks it was apparent that no one was prepared for an extended stay. We went out in almost a heatwave so the children hadn't brought any warm clothes with them. And then one morning there was a raid in Rushton, a village next to us, and the school was hit and three Colchester children and three local children were killed. That upset everybody and they all wanted to go home.

Nora Frost (born 1919)

I Was Buried Under the Timbers, Slates and Brick Chimney

Towards the end of 1943, there seemed to be a lull in the bombing of London and I returned home. Little did I know that six months later I would be a victim of one of the first flying bombs to fall on London. The bombing took place early one Sunday morning in June 1944. The bomb landed about a hundred yards away and our house was severely damaged by the blast. Unfortunately, I was asleep within the Mansard roof of the house and I ended up being buried under the timbers, slates and brick chimney, most of which thankfully missed me. After being dug out I was taken to St Bartholomew's Hospital, where I spent three days, suffering from concussion and having my wounds stitched up. My mother decided to send me back to Colchester and I found myself cycling to Aldersgate station (now the Barbican), with my case containing my worldly possessions balanced on the handlebars, and then to Liverpool Street for Colchester. Granny was surprised to see me as communications at the time were virtually non-existent.

Gordon Williams (born 1931)

Gordon Williams was a casualty of one of the first flying bombs to be dropped on London.

Holidays at Home

During the war years, holidays at the seaside were a thing of the past, but efforts were made to provide a programme of entertainment in the Castle Park under the banner, 'Holidays at Home'. These were based around the bandstand and included concert party shows, talent competitions and musical items, which were organised by 'Happy Harry' McCrae. I can also remember watching the Americans playing some baseball matches in the Lower Castle Park. There was also wartime entertainment at the Albert Hall in the High Street where a repertory company, under Bob Digby, presented a different play each week, and a pantomime at Christmas. When the company was having its summer break, and also as part of the Holidays at Home scheme, the Les Parcs Marionette Theatre performed at the Albert Hall. These marionettes were made and operated by Les Sparkes, who was the manager of the Co-operative Funeral Service Department. The name of the company 'Les Parcs', was obviously a play on his own name.

David Snow (born 1930)

There Was a Big Party in the Street

At the end of the war, we had the VE Day celebrations. There was a big party in the street, with everyone milling around and lots of noise and music. Bunting and flags hung on all the houses and stretched right across the road. On the corner of Charles Street and Kendall Road, outside the butcher's shop, somebody had dragged out a piano and everyone was dancing and very happy. I can remember *Roll Out the Barrel* being played over and over again.

Jacki Barber (born 1941)

A recent picture of David Snow and his wife, Janet.

Chapter Five

Horses & Trams

Riding in a Hansom Cab

I remember riding in a Hansom cab in London. It was quite comfortable and you sat in a little seat and a thing came over so that you were enclosed, and a man sat at the back. I can also remember the first motor car in Colchester and I saw it coming up East Hill. The owner used to keep it in a garage on a piece of land off Roman Road, and years later, when we had a car, we kept it in the same garage, for which we paid 5s a week rent. When the trams started, it was a treat to just get on board and go for a ride. And I remember one day when so many people crowded onto a tram that the driver refused to move until some of them got off. They went to North station and right up Crouch Street to Lexden.

Nellie Lissimore (born 1889)

It Was All Horses in Those Days

I can remember going up to London on one occasion with my uncle, and when we got there all the streets were cleared – it was all horses in those days – and a carriage came by and inside was Queen Victoria, sitting right up high, so that we could all see her. The Boer War had finished and I think that she was going to the House of Commons. I think that was the last time that she was out. I can also remember when I was going to school that they were putting the tramlines down, and I can remember years later them taking them up again. The trams went from near St Albright's in Stanway to the post office in Head Street. Some used to go to North station, and others went down High Street, St Botolph's Street and down to the Hythe. They started in 1904 and crowds of people watched.

Walter Barritt (born 1892)

There Were Not Many Cars Around

I remember Gen. Larpent, who used to live at Holmwood Lodge, Chitts Hill. He used to have a big carriage and pair and his livery men used to wear these cockade hats and they used to sit on the front of the carriage – they looked very smart. There was lots of horse traffic around when I was young, and there were not many cars. You might see the odd one but that was about it. I used to come into town with my grandfather in his horse and van. They used to have stables at the Cups Hotel, and at the Kings Arms for horses, and I believe also at the Bull Hotel. And, of course, there were no end of horses up at the Calvary Barracks.

Harry Salmon (born 1895)

A Hansom cab standing outside the King's Head inn at Lexden.

Motor Cars Were a Novelty

There weren't many motor cars around then, but if you heard one coming it was a novelty and you would rush out to see it. They only travelled about 15 mph and you often couldn't see much because of the dust, because they were gravel roads then. There were lots of horse-drawn vehicles around at that time. I remember the big old wagonettes. My mother and father, uncles and aunts and grandparents, at certain times, if they could afford it, would hire one and go to Clacton for the day. It would only cost them about a shilling each. They were drawn by two horses and it would be a real day out for them. I can also remember the old carriers. They used to come along the top here through Crockleford at a certain time, maybe about ten in the morning and they would come back about three in the afternoon, once or twice a week, and on a Saturday. One came from East Bergholt and one from Manningtree and they would do shopping for people. If you couldn't go to town, mother would send the children up to the top road to meet the carrier with a note to do some shopping for her – it cost about a penny. Then, of course, you had to be up there in the afternoon to meet him on the way home. They also used to carry passengers, maybe eight or nine people, sitting on ordinary wooden seats around the side of the cart. When they got to town, they would put up at the Castle pub, which had stables. They would take the horses out and feed them, leave them there while they went off to do the shopping for people and collect them again later in the day. The carriers were a great help to the people in the villages.

Arthur Went (born 1903)

Seats Either Side With Cushions

The carrier carts used to come from Great Oakley and Wix and would come along the Harwich Road through Elmstead to Colchester. They came in on Mondays, Wednesdays and Fridays and we would pick them up at Little Bentley and pay

Arthur Went, aged ninety-seven, pictured in 2000.

sixpence for a ride into Colchester. They were coloured carts, with boarded sides and a big frame over them. You got in through the front and the seats ran along either side with cushions on them, with room for about twelve passengers, six each side. We would meet the carrier at about ten o'clock and it would be between eleven and eleven thirty before they arrived in town. When they got to town, they would put up at the Castle pub and stable their horse in the yard. The carriers would take orders for people who wanted some shopping done, or perhaps wanted some special medicines from the chemist. And if you had anything to sell they would take it into the shops and bring the money back at night. They would make a small charge of tuppence or thruppence. If you wanted him, you had to be on the road because he would stop at certain places. The carrier never went out of his way, you had to be on his route.

Ethel Appleby (born 1901)

Picture of the Tram

I had my photo taken with the first tram that came up to the recreation ground – they never went any further than that. I had been on the 'Rec' with my friend Billy Woods and they were going to take a picture of this tram, so I said to Billy, 'Come on, they're going to take a picture of the tram, let's go and have our picture taken.' So we had our picture taken standing in the middle of the road, with the tram and the Recreation Hotel. And I remember that I'd got a red frock on with a black frill.

Margaret Golby (born 1901)

The Trams Had Wooden Seats

The streets were full of horses and carts in those days. And there would always be horse manure in the streets, which people would clear up for their gardens – it was never left in the road as there was always somebody after it. If it was outside your house, you had it. I can also remember the trams and they had wooden seats

In 1906, the town's tramway system was extended as far as the Recreation Ground in Old Heath Road. This picture was probably taken to commemorate the event and may also include young Margaret Golby and her friend Billy.

This view shows a tram approaching along East Bay en route to the High Street. Note the horse drinking trough at the junction with Brook Street and the sizeable crowd of young onlookers.

upstairs that you could fix to face the way that they were going. You would just swing the seat backwards or forwards. We all liked to get on top of the trams. If it rained there was a waterproof covering to go over your legs. They didn't go very fast, but faster than you could walk.

Doris Thimblethorpe (born 1903)

They Were Very Bumpy to Ride On

The trams used to go from the Recreation Ground up to town and down North Hill. They were very bumpy to ride on and they used to rattle and shake, especially up top because they were all open. When they got to the terminus, the driver had to get off and pull the overhead arm round and go the other way with it. They never went very fast – maybe about 10 mph, except when they went down North Hill and they forgot to put the brake on, then it would go quicker. The driver was in the front in all weathers – whether it was pouring with rain or not – because they were all open-fronted. He got the lot. The seats up top could be pushed forwards or backwards so that you always faced the front. I also remember that there used to a man named B– who lived in the same road as us and he worked for one of the brewing companies. Nine times out of ten he would come home through the streets with his horse and dray, and he would be blind drunk, and the horse would go right up to the house and stop there, and his wife used to come out and take him in.

Albert Bridges (born 1908)

Tramcar No. 6 seen approaching Lexden. The destination board at the front says 'Car Depot Only' and this may have been one of the early trial runs prior to the official opening.

To Clacton in an Open-Topped Charabanc

I had a great fear of the old tramlines. I used to cycle to school and if you got your wheel caught in the tramlines, you were almost sure to come off. One of the trickiest parts to negotiate was at the top of North Hill turning into High Street, because the tramlines went round the corner. It was always a fear that we might get caught. When the tram went under North Station bridge and you were sitting on the top, you had to be very careful to stay sitting because the bridge was very low. The back of the seats on the upper deck could be swung in either direction depending on which way the tram was travelling. I can also remember during the First World War going by motor bus down to West Mersea. There were two rival services, Berry's and the Primrose, and it cost about one shilling and sixpence return. When we went to Clacton we used to travel in a private charabanc, which was owned by Mr Rowles, who had his own little charabanc service at the bottom of East Hill. He had a garage down there. It was an open-topped vehicle with a hood, which could be pulled back in bad weather. I believe that he also ran a taxi service.

Alice Twyman (born 1906)

I Was Knocked Down by a Tram

I can remember being knocked down by a tram once. I was crossing the road outside Langley's cycle shop in Military Road, when this tram came along. The driver was attempting to stop and the 'cow catcher' on the front of the tram hit me. I shruck and wailed and old Langley came out, carried me home, and bandaged me up. I was more frightened than hurt.

Dick Thorogood (born 1911)

A Tram Ride to Lexden

I used to like going for a ride on the trams. They were very noisy and when they went down North Hill they had to pull up part way down and nearly stop; it was

Geoffrey Gunton still working in his Crouch Street shop in 1998, aged eighty-four.

a steep hill and the brakes weren't strong enough to hold them if they went straight down. The seats on top were made of iron and you could swing the back of the seat backwards or forwards according to which way they were going. I remember quite a few times being on them and they would have to stop. I don't know what went wrong, but the seats would get hot. On one occasion when the seat got hot we all had to get up and we could see steam coming out. Then it started up again and away we went. They never went very fast – probably no more than 20 mph, probably less than that. They were open-topped and you had to go downstairs if it rained, or else take an umbrella with you. I remember on one August bank holiday, father and mother taking us seven or eight children on a tram ride to Lexden. When we got there we had a picnic at Lexden Gravel Pit, where there were blackberries growing, and then came home again. We used to look forward to these occasions. Pleasures were simple in those days, but we enjoyed them.

Geoffrey Gunton (born 1914)

Everyone Walked in Lexden Road

If we needed to catch a tram to town, we would go to the bottom of North Hill, where they stopped near the market. There was a line going up the hill and one coming down, and they never went further than North station. We often used to take the children for a tram ride to Lexden on a Sunday evening. We had to go to the top of North Hill and into the High Street, before catching a tram to Lexden that came up the High Street, then round into Head Street and out that way. We would probably take the tram out to Lexden and then walk home. Everyone walked in Lexden Road on a Sunday evening. When the bypass route was opened ,everyone walked along there. The seats on the trams were like cane with lots of holes in it. They were open-topped and on the seat in front of you there was a cover that you just lifted off and pulled it over yourself, which kept the water off your lap.

Ethel Appleby (born 1901)

This charming view of Lexden Road in the early 1900s shows a tram en route to Lexden and a returning tram approaching from the opposite direction. Lexden Road was a popular location for taking a walk – either as a courting couple or perhaps as a family.

Chapter Six

People, Leisure & Events

She Looked as Yellow as a Guinea

I remember Emma and Grimes very well. I was going home from work one night when I saw them both. Grimes was standing by the side of the road and Emma was lying in a shop doorway. And I asked how they were and Emma looked as yellow as a guinea. I said to Grimes, 'Where are you going to sleep tonight?' And he said, 'Well, if I had a shilling, we could sleep at the common lodging house in Vineyard Street,' So I gave him a shilling and then he said to me, 'Emma wants some butter.' So I told that I didn't have any butter and went to cross the road. As I did so, a policeman called out to me, 'You've just given our friends some money haven't you?' I said that I had and he said, 'Well look where they are going.' And they were shuffling their way into the tobacconist shop to buy some snuff. And on the corner of St Botolph's Street and Priory Street, there used to be a confectionary shop called Wash's, so I went in and said to the lady that Grimes says that Emma wants some butter. And she said to me, 'My dear, I can't give you a piece of butter, but I can give you a pile of bread and butter that's been left over from the teas. So I took it to Grimes and then I went home. When I went to work in the morning,

Marmalade Emma and Teddy Grimes were well known local tramps in the early years of the twentieth century. Note that Emma is enjoying a smoke from her clay pipe.

Grimes was waiting for me and he said, 'Emma didn't want bread and butter and she died last night.' And he was already wearing a black armband.

Nellie Lissimore (born 1889)

It Was a Wonderful Sight

I can remember attending the pageant in 1909 and I thought it was a wonderful sight, to see all these historical people out there dressed in medieval costumes. In that day we thought it was a wonderful thing. I remember that quite a lot of the townsfolk were in the pageant, including one lady, Miss Alfreda Sanders. I remember it quite well.

Harry Salmon (born 1985)

I Was in the Rigadoon Dance

I took part in the Colchester Pageant in 1909. I was in the Rigadoon Dance and my partner was a boy named Welham. I can remember us twirling around and there were hundreds of people there every day. I wore a two-colour dress and had my photograph taken. There were lots of marquees with photographs and refreshments and we could just go in at any time and have what we wanted. I don't remember how I was chosen to take part in the pageant, but I do remember my father taking me somewhere for rehearsals. My costume was terracotta and orange in colour, and was all in points with a bell on the end. I also wore odd shoes and socks, one of one colour and one another. I have only happy memories of the pageant.

Dorothy Lawrence (born 1897)

Children from the Bluecoat Central School in their pageant costumes. Note that three of the children are dressed as Rigadoon dancers, as evidencd by their two-pointed hats with small bells attached.

We Had to Cross the Road by Boat

At the time of the floods in 1953, I was sent down to Jaywick and the place was full of water. We couldn't walk across the road – we had to cross the road by boat. We went round the different villas in a boat to see if anyone was in them. And we pulled out one dead man. The water was 5 or 6 feet deep.

Geoff Beddall (born 1902)

The Police Station Has Been Flooded

On the night of the 1953 floods, we had been down to Clacton to an old time dance, and when we came back I was intending to go up Hythe Hill and into town. Well we got as far as the Co-op coal yard in Hythe Station Road when a car stopped in front of me. And he said to me, 'You won't get any further, the road is flooded.' So we went home by a different route. The next morning I went up to the station and they said to me, 'You're going down to Harwich – the police station has been flooded.' So we went down there and I just couldn't believe my eyes when I saw the floods there. The police station was totally flooded – cars were covered with water and everything. We spent the whole day down there and I remember we had a rowing boat to go round the streets. And I remember that one of the Co-op horses had got itself stuck in the hallway of a house and we thought, how the hell are we going to get him out of there? Eventually, we managed to back him out by making a bit of noise by banging on the window and then the Co-op people came and took him away. I've never seen so much devastation in my life. When the water eventually went down there was mud everywhere.

Bill Geddes (born 1905)

We Would Go Walking in the High Street

Girls and boys would often meet up with each other walking along the High Street. I remember on one occasion, when I was about eighteen, my friend and

Mann's music shop as seen around 1900. The firm has been trading from this same High Street location since 1891, although the business was established in 1854 by Frederick Mann, the great-great-grandfather of the current managing director Tim Mann. Note also the early motor car parked outside the shop.

I were walking along the High Street one Saturday evening and we stopped and spoke to some boys who asked if we'd like to go for a walk together. So we went for a walk through the park and then along Lexden Road. I wasn't allowed out much on my own, except perhaps on a Sunday after church. I had to attend church three times on a Sunday and when I came out of church, I would always take the long way round to get home. I met my husband George in the High Street – I was with my friend and we met these two boys. We were introduced and we went for a walk together through the park and down the back and round to home. I was about twenty-one at the time and we were courting for about five years before we got married. When we got married we lived in Crowhurst Road. There was no bathroom but someone gave us a long tin bath as a wedding present. We used to put it in the kitchen and heat the water up in the copper, or if not in kettles and saucepans. To start with we had a kitchen range to do the cooking, but later had a gas stove put in. We had to pay about a shilling a week rent for it. I don't think that anyone bought gas stoves in those days.

Doris Thimblethorpe (born 1903)

I Still Play the Violin Every Sunday
When I was about seventeen I said to my brother Ernie, 'I'm going up town tonight to but a violin', so Ernie said that he would as well. So we went to Mann's music shop in the High Street and I selected one that cost two pounds, and Ernie's was one pound ten shillings. So we bought them with their cases and bows and brought them home. We hadn't told dad that we were going to buy them and he said to us, 'What are you going to do with them?' And we said, 'Play them of course', and dad said, 'You never will.' So we were so determined to learn how to play our violins that one of our uncles who lived nearby said that he would help us with the fingering and play a tune. So every night we would get upstairs – you couldn't do it downstairs, learning a violin is

This view shows crowds of Edwardian children queuing up for entry to the Saturday morning picture show at the Vaudeville cinema, kown as the 'Penny Rush' (the cinema was later renamed the Empire).

like a cat on the tiles – we used to go up there and fiddle away every night. Our uncle would see how we were getting on and give us another one to learn. We learned to play on what you call a two flat tune, and then went on to an E and a B. Dad could hear us playing upstairs and one day he said, 'Bring them downstairs and I'll play with you,' Dad had a brass instrument so we played together and uncle, who was also the Sunday school superintendent, told us to bring our violins to Sunday school and play them. And we're still both playing our violins at the chapel over seventy years later.

Arthur Went (born 1903)

The Old Days Were Better

We used to get our toys and things at Moore and Roberts in Buttles Street (St Botolph's Street). Next door was Hancock's where we used to get a ha'penny bag of sweets. Further down was a greengrocer's, where we could buy a pennyworth of mixed fruit. On Saturday mornings as children we'd all go to the Vaudeville, where we would stand and wait for the doors to open. We called it the 'Penny Rush' and there would often be two or three rats running about in there. We had a lovely time. When we came out we would walk home along the moors and have a friendly fight with friends on the way. I definitely think that the old days were better. I was poor compared to what I have now. We were very poor, but respectfully poor. I can't explain what I mean by that, but we were not rough, we were not allowed to go running the streets and swearing, or anything like that. The children in those days all mucked in and played together, but everybody is well off today.

Elsie Seaborne (born 1908)

We Would Go in the Front Room and Sing Hymns

We never had a television or anything like that but dad used to play his piano. And on Sundays, we would go into the front room and sing hymns. We didn't have electricity and had gas lighting. When I got older, we would always go out dancing wherever there was a dance. They used to have dances in the Co-op Hall and they would have a band. I also belonged to the Sons of Temperance and they used to meet in Osborne Street.

Doris Lawson (born 1908)

We Used to Play in the Streets

We had no television or radio when we were young, so to amuse ourselves we used to play in the streets – rounders or football – it was safe enough to play in the streets in those days. And there were all manner of people that used to come round the streets. There used to be these acrobats, and poor old Captain Slasher. He used to walk drawing one leg behind the other in the gutter with a tin whistle. He was from the First World War and didn't know what to do, so he would play this tin whistle and then put his hat round. Another character was Tom Piper. He always used to run in front of the tram when it started up, and then there was Manhole Kate, who every time that she saw a manhole she used to dance up and down on it.

Albert Bridges (born 1908)

Skipping in the Park

We used to go skipping in the park on Good Fridays. There used to be no end of soldiers down there who were always in uniform. We used to all mix together and they would have these great long ropes and anyone could join in. I can't remember not being there on a Good Friday. We had to go to church on Sunday mornings, Sunday school in the afternoon and church again at night. That was at St Mary Magdalen and next door to the church was a baker's shop run by a man named Fletcher. One day he told my father that I had been misbehaving in church and I got a telling off for that. We had special shoes and clothes set aside for Sundays. I don't remember my mother and father ever going to church, although they wouldn't let us do any work on that day except read. It was the Sabbath day and you were not allowed to do anything. My mother wouldn't do any washing or anything. On Sunday afternoons, when we came home from Sunday school, we would all go for a walk. Families did a lot of walking in those days.

Dorothy Lawrence (born 1897)

People Want So Much Today

When we first got married we had a wireless. You made it yourself, or somebody made it for you. And we also had a gramophone. There were no washing machines in those days and you had to do everything by hand. Everybody was in the same boat. You swept the floors and polished them – there were no vacuum cleaners. Looking back, people want so much today and are never satisfied. We never had any trouble in those days, we never heard of so much crime. You could leave your house open, or could walk about with your money in your hand, and never had to worry about your purse. I still go to church on Sundays. I also attend a social club once a fortnight. I am usually knitting from morn to night. I knit for the hospice – they bring me the wool, new or old, and I make what I like from it. I make all sorts of things, including shawls, baby's things, gloves, bed socks, blankets, cushions and tea cosies. I never stop. And it's all voluntary; I never get paid for anything.

Doris Thimblethorpe (born 1903)

This view shows some of the marching military bands outside the Camp church on Military Road. Listening to the bands playing on the parade ground was a popular pastime on Sunday mornings.

There Would Be About 1,000 People There

On Sunday mornings, we used to go up to the Camp on Military Road. All the bands from the different regiments used to play on the parade ground before marching to Camp church. The Foot Regiment used to march very fast, about 140 steps to the minute, and then the artillery regiments would walk very slowly. The regiments all had their own bands and when it was over, there would be one band left in the square and they would play to all the people. I would say that there were about 1,000 people up there at a time.

Albert Bridges (born 1908)

We Played With Our Tops and Hoops

At Christmas, we would get a sixpenny toy from Woolworths and an apple and orange in our stocking. Birthdays were the same as any other day. When I was at school we used to play with our tops and hoops. I had a wooden hoop – only the people with money had the iron ones. Another thing we did was to get a key with a hollow end, take a red match (Swan Vesta), put the head of the match in the key, tie a nail to the key with a length of string, put the nail in the key and then swing the key against a wall. It gave a good bang. In the evening we would play board games, and in the summer we would go over the Wick (Middlewick Ranges) and play cowboys and Indians and make bows and arrows. I also used to go fishing in the Castle Park for newts and tiddlers. I never had a bicycle when I was young as we couldn't afford it.

Dick Thorogood (born 1911)

We Used to Play Party Games

At Christmas time, we used to decorate the house with homemade trimmings and play party games. With one game you would get a hot plate and put some raisins all over it, get it very hot, then pour some whisky or brandy on it, and then set it alight. We would then put the lights out and pick them up and eat them. You could see the light go right to your mouth and it didn't burn to pick them up. We used to call that game Snapdragon.

Albert Hewitt (born 1903)

Chicken Was a Special Treat in Those Days

At Christmas time, I had to stone the raisins and chop up the candied peel for my mother to make the mincemeat. We had a happy time at Christmas. We would put up a few decorations, mainly paper chains and holly. And we would have chicken for Christmas dinner, which was a special treat in those days. And I can remember, on one occasion, my mother and father going out shopping and then there being a knock on the door and there was this shopkeeper standing there with all the Christmas presents, which we weren't supposed to see. I used to have to be in bed by eight o'clock, but my father used to play games with us. As soon as we had finished tea, we children used to sit round the table with my father and he would play cards with us until it was time for us to go to bed. There would be a hanging oil lamp over the table, but we had to take a candle and candlestick to bed.

Dorothy Lawrence (born 1897)

I Used to Make Brass Ornaments

We built our house here in D'arcy Road in 1935. We paid £70 for the ground (54 feet wide and 160 feet long), and it cost us £400 to build. And we paid £14 for our

Albert Bridges, aged eighty-four, in 1992.

first bedroom suite, although in those days I was only earning £2 8s a week. In my later years, I used to spend a lot of time making brass ornaments. I used to make them from bar brass, which I used to get from Martin and Parnell's on North Hill. And when they closed I used to go round to Wheeler's scrap merchants and get what I wanted from them. It used to cost me a few pounds. The most difficult model I made was of a tramp sitting on a bench, with a little dog sitting by his side and with a little saddlebag on the seat with his belongings in. And he is holding a piece of bread in one hand, and a fork with a sausage on it in the other. I started by getting a piece of copper sheet and made the seat first, and then I started on the figure. I started on the body and then the legs, arms, hands and head are all separate. Everything was carefully silver-soldered together. I made a jacket, trousers and boots all separately. One of the hardest jobs was making the jacket. I had to cut it out to make it look like a jacket and put the lapels on – because it was a solid piece until I filed it all down. I also made the little sandwich and the dog separately. I can't say how long it took to make one – maybe 500 hours on and off, from time to time.

Albert Bridges (born 1908)

Children's Christmas Breakfast
We once went to the Poor Children's Christmas Breakfast in the Corn Exchange. Inside we played games and sang carols. I remember doing that because when I started singing one of the children who was sitting next to me gave me a push and said, 'You ain't got to shout like that.' And I remember going and telling my mother about it, and how they told us to sing, and she said, 'No dear, you did right.' We were all given a new penny and an orange and apple.

Elsie Seabourne (born 1908)

We Used to Swim in the River

On Saturday mornings we used to go to the pictures at the Empire (previously the Vaudeville) on Mersea Road. All the kids used to go there and it only cost a penny. The films were all about heroes and villains, or Tarzan. Sometimes you would get hit in the back of the neck by someone throwing an ice cream. I also used to go to the Headgate Theatre, where I remember seeing the first talking picture. Before that, there would be someone playing the piano while the film was on. When I got older, I used to belong to the swimming club. There was a bathing place down by the river before the open-air pool was built. It was where the river had a sandy bottom and they used to have these little changing huts with a half door. We were actually swimming in the river and we used to pay about tuppence a time. Before breakfast on a Sunday morning, about six o'clock, five of us would go down the bathing place for a swim, then we'd come home and have breakfast before getting on our bikes and cycling to Clacton, have another swim, then a cup of coffee, and then cycle back for dinner.

Dick Thorogood (born 1911)

The Front Room Was Transformed

Christmas was a special day, when the front room was transformed and the contents hidden away with paper chains, holly and other trimmings. We would have a large Christmas tree in the window with lots of candles on it – quite dangerous, but it never caught fire. Preparations began in the early autumn with payments to the slate club, and as time went by the goodies were collected. Nuts, oranges, hams, beef and wines and spirits. This was the only time that my father bought whisky at 3s 6d a bottle. We also had no television in those days and the wireless was still in its early stages. So our main form of entertainment would be the cinema. For fivepence you could sit through two shows in the front row with your head tilted back as far as it would go in order to read the caption on the screen, such as 'Night fell, but no one was injured.' The musical accompaniment was provided by a harmonium, which must have been hard work for the player.

Les Beagen (born 1910)

We Used to Go Bird Nesting

One of my pastimes when I was young would be to go bird nesting with one or two friends. Whenever we found a nest we would count how many eggs there were and would never take any if there were only one or two. But if there were three or four eggs in there, we would take one for our collection. We would then make a little hole at either end of the egg and then blow through one end, holding the egg very carefully, and the white and yolk would come out at the other end. We would then label them and pack them in cotton wool in an old Oxo tin. I must have had about fifty or sixty different eggs, all collected from trees and quarries in the area. The one that I was most proud of was an owl's egg. I also collected cigarette cards when I was at school. We would swap them with other boys in order to complete our sets. At playtime, two or more boys would play with their cards by flicking them up against a wall with the most skilful winning all the cards. You would either win a lot of cards, or lose a lot. We used to beg for cards from people we knew who smoked, and if we saw someone opening a packet of cigarettes in the street we would go up and ask for the cigarette card.

Basil Smith (born 1924)

We Used to Make Our Own Entertainment

For entertainment at home we had a radio, which, if you fiddled with it, you could pick up stations from places such as Germany and France. Other than that we used to make our own entertainment. As we got a little older we got into things like comics, and you would end up with a great big pile of them. And very often one of your friends would come knocking on your door wanting to swap comics, so we would sit at the table and exchange them. We were also quite fortunate in that we lived just a short distance from the Wick and you could always get a football game going, or perhaps a game of cricket.

Hugh Harvey (born 1932)

A Carefree Childhood

We had a carefree childhood playing in the streets, with children of all ages playing together. A particular favourite was to follow a trail of clues. The oldest boy in the road used to hide tiny paper clues over a long course in the New Town area, and it could take an hour or more to follow the trail – we loved playing that game. We used to stay out until it got quite dark and the signal for us to go home in the winter was the sight of the lamplighter coming to switch on the gas street light. In 1947, there was a big freeze. The snow was piled up in our street so high that we had to dig a channel from the front door across the path to the road. To us kids it was fantastic. We had the most marvellous ice slides, which were worked on until they were like glass, and we became quite expert at sliding almost a quarter of the way down the street. We all used to line up to take our turn, and even some of the adults joined in.

Jacki Barber (born 1941)

Five Cinemas in the Town

We had five cinemas in the town. There was the Regal in Crouch Street, the Headgate (Cameo), the Playhouse in St John's Street, the Hippodrome in the High Street and the Empire at the bottom of Mersea Road. More often than not you

Hugh Harvey, pictured in 2013, aged eighty-one.

Above left: The Hippodrome was a popular venue for entertainment in the town, first as a music hall and variety theatre and later as a cinema.

Above right: Jacki Barber, pictured in December 2013.

would have to queue to get in, particularly on a Saturday, and a commissionaire (dressed in a smart uniform) would be employed to control the queue. The programme of films being shown would include a major film, a second feature, a newsreel and possibly one or two cartoons making a programme lasting about three hours. This programme would be shown continuously and you could choose to come and go when you wished, and even see the programme through more than once.

David Snow (1930)

Coronation Street Party

I can remember the Queen's Coronation. My uncle, who lived in North Station Road, had a television and I can remember us going down there to watch the Queen's Coronation on television, and it poured with rain. And some of the neighbours in the road also came in to watch it. We had a street party here in Cavendish Avenue down the centre of the road and we all sat there eating. Later on, I can remember there being music played, with the adults dancing in the road until late at night, although we children, of course, had been packed off to bed by then.

Jill Thorogood (born 1943)

A scene from the 1953 Coronation tea party in Cavandish Avenue. Jill Thorogood can be seen seated in the front row, fifth from the left, in her gypsy costume.

People Were Jammed in Like Sardines

I can remember the time when Colchester played Huddersfield Town in the FA Cup in 1948. I took a young friend along with me and we managed to shin up a drainpipe and stood on top of the gents' toilets to watch the game. It was a stupid thing to do because it was only pieces of corrugated iron. There were about 16,000 people crammed into the ground. They were perched on trees and anywhere else where you could get a view of the pitch. People were jammed like sardines in there. A lot of the Colchester players at that time were only part-timers, but we had some good players such as 'Digger' Kettle, Len Cater and Arthur Turner. The footballers in those days were all well known to everyone and you would perhaps meet them in the town. Huddersfield had several stars and internationals playing for them and we were expecting to be hammered about 5-0. When the game started, the U's seemed to be holding their own and by half time it was still 0-0. And then with about 20 minutes to go, with the U's pressing at the far end of the pitch from where we were, we heard a terrific roar and we realised that Colchester had scored. A player called Bob Curry had put the ball into the net and we were 1-0 up. The crowd were shouting and screaming but the worst part was that we still had about 20 minutes to go. It would have been lovely if it had been the last minute, but for us it seemed like the longest twenty minutes you could imagine. As the game drew to a close, Huddersfield were running rings around us. They hit the post, the crossbar and they did everything but score. And then at the final whistle the whole place erupted and there were celebrations in the town. Everybody streamed out of the ground in a good mood

Colchester United supporters cheer on their team as they dump Huddesfield Town out of the FA Cup in 1948.

and were talking about it all the time. It was the first time that a non-league club had beaten a league club since before the war.

Hugh Harvey (born 1932)

Skipping in the Park
In the summer months, a favourite game used to be skipping. A large rope would be stretched across the whole width of the road and would be turned by two of the oldest kids. At Easter time, we used to go to the park with our skipping ropes – it was a traditional event. Good Friday was not only a day for hot cross buns, but also for skipping. There was usually a good turn out with skipping ropes of all sizes. I longed to join in with the big rope, but only the bigger girls got the chance, and by the time I was big enough the tradition seemed to have disappeared.

Jacki Barber (born 1941)

A Very Friendly Atmosphere
Everybody in the neighbourhood knew each other and it was a very friendly atmosphere. Each year after the war, the publican of the Blue Boar public house used to organise a coach trip to Southend to see the lights being switched on. Everybody went, including the children, and it was a day out that was very much looked forward to as few people had cars of their own at that time. Apart from the odd trip to the seaside by train we never went away on holiday, but then neither did anyone else so we didn't feel as though we were missing out on anything.

Jacki Barber (born 1941)

We Called it the Disc Club
Sometime around 1966, a friend of mine called Terry Hann and I were looking for a place somewhere locally to use as a live music venue. We had previously been using St Leonard's Village Hall down the Hythe, but we now needed something more

suitable and closer to town. And we finally found what we were looking for. It was ideal really because it was right in the middle of town, just off the High Street, with fewer neighbours to worry about, and this was St Martin's church in West Stockwell Street. The building had been deconsecrated as a church and was being used as a hall known as St Martin's Centre. At the time, it was being used by an amateur dramatic society for their rehearsals and productions, and they had built a stage at one end, there was power laid on and toilets available, and there was also a little cafeteria that had been set up in the old vestry, so it was ideal for us. So we took it on and we called it the Disc Club. We held the main event with a live group on a Saturday night, and if you kept your ticket you could get in for free on a Monday evening when we would just play records. We had to keep a strict note of all the records that we played, and how many times we played them, which we then had to submit to the various different bodies who were responsible for copyright on recorded material, because we were making money out of somebody else's property as such. The building was licensed to hold 250 people, although on one occasion we hired a popular group from Sudbury who had their own large following of fans, and about five or six coachloads of these supporters turned up on the night. And on that one occasion we had nearly 500 people in the hall. We also had to employ bouncers on the door to ensure that we didn't get any riff-raff in and to check that people weren't trying to gain free entry via the fire exits, because these had to be kept unlocked. We catered for an age range of between about sixteen and twenty-one and we never sold any alcohol, although drinking alcohol didn't seem to feature as much in those days as it does now. People were generally happy enough with a Coke or an orange and perhaps a bag of crisps. We always had a group on a Saturday night and we used to get some fairly well-known bands performing there, as well as one or two

St Martin's church in West Stockwell Street was the unlikely venue for the Disc Club in the 1960s.

famous people turning up including, on one occasion, Screaming Lord Such. We would probably have to pay the group anything up to about £120, which was quite good money at the time. Of course, many of the really good groups were way out of our price range, so it was fairly low-key stuff. We had to be out of the building, lock stock and barrel, by midnight, so by about 11.15 p.m. everything started to shut down and by 11.30 p.m. it was over, leaving us just half an hour to clean up, sweep up and get all our equipment out.

Fred Rayner (born 1947)

Fred Rayner and his friend Terry Hann, pictured together in July 1969, on the occasion of Fred's marriage to his fiancée Cherry Bryan.